Smart Read Easy

This child centred, simple route to reading for pre-school children has been tried and tested with great success over a number of years by the author, a psychology graduate and qualified teacher. The scheme, an amalgamation of sight reading and the currently favoured synthetic systematic phonics approach, encourages children to learn to read with Sam, a character they will find fun and very easy to identify with.

This scheme allows children to create their own first reading book which is followed by a series of fifteen short stories gradually extending most frequently used words to include the 45 key words to reading advised by the National Literacy Strategy. With pictures to colour and space for drawing, there is plenty of scope for children to have fun making this book their own.

With no punishing schedules to follow, this all inclusive activity book offers a very flexible approach, ensuring an enjoyable and satisfying reading adventure for both you and your child.

This book is dedicated
to
Bridget Jane GILL, (JEAN)
Former Officer-in-Charge, Parkview Private Pre-School

'When Irish Eyes are Smiling'
a tribute to Bridget Jane GILL, (JEAN)

Originally from Galway in Southern Ireland, Jean, upon retiring from secondary school teaching, joined us shortly after we opened. There were many applicants for the post and after the final round of interviews I had no doubt in my mind as to whom I wanted to appoint.

This lovely lady with her lashings of Irish charm, always cheerful, always friendly, helpful and wise. Jean with her twinkling brown eyes and wonderful sense of humour. Reliable Jean, dependable Jean, who as far as I can recall, never had a day off in all the time she was there. Jean was a dream appointment. A wonderful, born teacher; she loved the children, taught them, laughed and sang with them, all the time caring about them whilst caring for them. Many children passed through our hands over the years and without exception they loved her dearly, as did their parents and Staff. Jean was an absolute gem. I wish I could go back and tell her so again, though thankfully we kept in touch and I never ceased to remind her just how much she was valued by us all. I, like others, started to feel very concerned when the contact ceased and it was with great sadness we learned of her death on 28th January 2012.

Jean's generous spirit fed into the local community, with her ongoing charity work and constant, willing help to those in need around her. Without doubt she will be sadly missed, not only by her family but by all who knew her. Always we will remember her with love and gratitude.

Margaret

Smart Read Easy

An informal, balanced approach to
the introduction of reading

Margaret Henderson Smith
BA., BA.(Hons.), Cert. Ed., MBPsS

Illustrated by the author (with the exception of the alphabet)
and
Rose, Anna, and Lucy Williams

Published 2013 by Abramis academic publishing

www.abramis.co.uk

ISBN 978 1 84549 575 6

© Margaret Henderson Smith 2013

All rights reserved

This book is copyright. Subject to statutory exception and to provisions of relevant collective licensing agreements, no part of this publication may be reproduced, stored in a retrieval system, or transmitted in any form or by any means, without the prior written permission of the author.

Printed and bound in the United Kingdom

This book is sold subject to the conditions that it shall not, by way of trade or otherwise, be lent, re-sold, hired out, or otherwise circulated without the publisher's prior consent in any form of binding or cover other than that which it is published and without a similar condition including this condition being imposed on the subsequent purchaser.

In the stories, the characters, places and events are either the product of the author's imagination or they are used entirely fictitiously. Any resemblance to actual persons, living or dead, is purely coincidental.

Abramis is an imprint of arima publishing.

arima publishing
ASK House, Northgate Avenue
Bury St Edmunds, Suffolk IP32 6BB
t: (+44) 01284 700321

Also For
Jack, Rose, Anna and Lucy
with love

Margaret Henderson Smith has also written 'The Harriet Series' of novels published by arima publishing:

A Question of Answers
Ne Obliviscaris: Do Not Forget
San Marco the End of the Road
Amber

also

A Flight of Fancy: A collection of Writings from The Big 40 Blog

Contact via websites:
www.margarethendersonsmith.co.uk
www.aquestionofanswers.com

Join me on Twitter @Maryroseanna

Contents

Foreword 1

Introduction 11

Sam 17

    My Alphabet Book

Getting started 39

My Reading Book 45

What's next? 157

    Book 1: Where is Sam's ball?

    Book 2: Sam's Cat

    Book 3: What Orange Pip Likes

    Book 4: Sam Goes on the Computer

    Book 5: Sam Teaches Orange Pip to Read

    Book 6: Orange Pip is a Very Bad Cat

    Book 7: Orange Pip Runs Away

    Book 8: Orange Pip Hides in the Tree

    Book 9: Orange Pip is a Good Cat Now

    Book 10: Sam is Happy

Second series work guide 159

    Book 11: All About Sam

    Book 12: Where Sam Lives

    Book 13: All About the Park

    Book 14: Sam Goes to the Park

    Book 15: Sam Gets into Trouble

Sam and Billy Ball 163

Flashcard wordlist 181

Flashcards for cutting 199

Flashcard blanks 301

References 309

Notes 311

Foreword

It is useful to place a reading scheme such as this into context for it is important to be aware of the current approach to the development of early literacy skills and the teaching methods used in primary schools. These have been guided by the non-statutory National Literacy Strategy introduced into English state schools in 1997 as a result of concerns about standards in primary schools, highlighted by Ofsted[1] and others. According to the House of Commons Eighth Report of Session 2004-05[2], whilst the NLS (now integrated with the Primary National Strategy) produced a significant improvement in reading standards, nevertheless findings supported by the PIRLS[3], from national tests[4] showed around 20% of children not to be reading to age at 11 yrs. Indeed, the report questions the reliability of the figures stated, in that some challenge the performance measure relating to these Government Key Stage 2 tests, suspecting teachers of "teaching to the test" and thereby producing inflated results.

Being non-statutory, the NLS has given free rein to schools to adopt their own teaching of reading strategies, though the HC Eighth Report referred to above found evidence to suggest pressure from Local Education Authorities and others for

---

[1] The Teaching of Reading in 45 Inner London Primary Schools. Ofsted, HMR 27/96/DS, 1 October 1996

[2] House of Commons Education and Skills Committee: Teaching Children to Read: Eighth Report of Session 2004-05: HC 121 Incorporating HC1269-I from Session 2003-04. Published 2005: House of Commons, London: The Stationery Office Limited

[3] The Progress in International Reading Literacy Study 2001

[4] A Reading Revolution: How we can teach every child to read, Preliminary Report of the Literacy Task Force, chaired by Professor Michael Barber: 27/02/97

schools to conform to the National Literacy Strategy by using the approved related schemes of work to facilitate what the above report refers to as the "searchlights" teaching method where a range of strategies drawing on the child's total experience generally come into play without specific emphasis on any one at any particular time. Thus, a child brings his/her own knowledge and experience of the world to the four "searchlights" tools identified in learning to read. Here we are looking at word recognition/graphic knowledge, grammatical knowledge, knowledge of context and an understanding of phonics, thereby enabling the teacher to employ one or more of these strategies in getting the child to work out the word. Of all these approaches, it would seem, the teaching of phonics has been the most closely scrutinised.

Let's draw out the phonics debate a little in relation to preschool children as there are differing theoretical approaches to the understanding of language development. Others outside this Report deserve a mention here. Katherine Demopoulos in writing for The Guardian "Children 'need 100 key words' to read" (www.guardian.co.uk/education/2005/dec/09/research.higher.education) states, under the direction of Dr. Jonathan Solity, researchers from Warwick University found children needed to learn only 100 words and 61 phonic skills, considerably less on both counts than those suggested by the NLS. Dr. Solity says these are the optimum number of sight skills and phonic skills needed to read. The researchers say the NLS teaches too many phonemes which are infrequently used eg. "dge" as in "fridge" and Dr. Solity suggests children would be better off learning such infrequently occurring sound clusters for themselves as they encounter them.

It is interesting to look at Baddley's tri-partite model (1986) of working memory which includes the phonological loop, a developmental cognitive facility which increases its storage capacity as a result of silent speech rehearsal. Research shows, (Baddeley, Thomson & Buchanan (1974)) pre-school children do not use this strategy but rely on images to aid recall. Their findings show by the age of 7 years children begin to use silent repetition as an aid to recall. In support of this Gathercole in 'The Structure and functioning of phonological short-term memory,

(Susan E. Gathercole, University of Bristol, England n.d.) finds memory storage capacity limits complex comprehension processes in children below the age of four years. Later findings show a link between vocabulary knowledge and phonological storage capacity at 4 - 5 yrs of age. This research shows, 'As memory capabilities tend to increase with age so does the ability to learn more complex vocabulary:' (Gathercole, S.E; Willis, C.S.; Emslie, H.; Baddeley, A.D. (1992) 'Phonological memory and vocabulary development during early school years: A longitudinal study'. Developmental Psychology 28.) in learning to read.)

For those interested in the physiological workings of the brain in relation to reading, I recommend the online publication which is a comprehensive analysis of language and reading by Professor Rosemary Sage, Professor and Dean of the College of Teachers, entitled: 'Not Just Phonics? Looking at Reading in the Context of a Phonic Emphases in Teaching' in which she concludes: '…we all learn differently and what is a successful approach for one person may not be so for another.' (http://www.collegeofteachers.ac.uk/news/not-just-phonics-)

The Report, The Early Childhood Foundation considers phonics teaching to be inappropriate for children in pre-school or reception classes saying it depends on the accurate pronunciation of letter names and presented with words out of context or uninteresting they may not be internalised into their knowledge base. (HC, Teaching Children to Read: Eighth Report of Session 2004-05: The Stationery Office Limited 2005: Section 4:62). Again Dr. Kevan Collins, Director of the National Primary Strategy informed the Report that phonics should not be taught in isolation and he did not feel the phonics programmes produce better readers, rather he says they show the level of phonic knowledge retention, but don't demonstrate the learning of other knowledge key to reading including context and syntax. He also felt controlling the reading environment by limiting texts to a child's existing phonological knowledge to be counter-productive and suggests strategies should be in place that would allow for the child to develop a confident and positive approach to all aspects of reading opportunities as they naturally occur in the environment. (HC, Teaching

Children to Read: Eighth Report of Session 2004-05: The Stationery Office Limited 2005: Section 3:28, 29).

Thus not all professional opinion, or one feels, research in this field would necessarily support the synthetic phonics approach to the teaching of reading currently favoured by the DfES.

Since its inception and in light of research and academic evidence the NLS has been continuously revised with particular emphasis on the teaching of phonics. In 2005 the Education and Skills Committee recommended that the DfES commission a large-scale study, comparing the National Literacy Strategy including the "searchlights" model with synthetic phonics (fast and first), analytical phonics and other methods. This Report draws on a broad spectrum of sometimes conflicting evidence and opinion and the findings conclude that in seeking to achieve the optimum methodology for the teaching of reading many (stated) existing variables be incorporated into the proposed comparative study, which, unfortunately never happened. Instead the DfES asked Jim Rose[5] to conduct an independent review of teaching of early reading; the results of which showed the need for the teaching of reading to focus on both word recognition and language comprehension. He proposed that this 'simple view of reading' replace the 'searchlights model' proposed by the NLS (later the Primary National Strategy). Also his findings were overwhelmingly in favour of the synthetic approach to systematic phonics as the prime means of deciphering the written word. As a result, the government's White Paper, 'The importance of teaching, Nov.2010' proposed this and the core criteria governing this is now incorporated into the new Teachers' Standards (DfE V1.0 0711, DfE 2011) which was implemented in September 2012.

---

[5] J. Rose: Independent review of the teaching of early reading: final report (0201-2006DOC-EN) DfES 20066 House of Commons: Education and Skills Committee: Teaching Children to Read: Eighth Report of Session 2004-05. Page 36, Paragraph 2.

One assumes the sheer cost of executing a large-scale comparative study between the approaches of the National Literacy Strategy and 'phonics fast and first' would have proved prohibitive and too time consuming when it was felt there was the need to act quickly to address the problem of the unacceptably high percentage of under-achieving readers at age 11 yrs. One feels this to be most unfortunate since some of the research cited suggests the cognitive ability to retain, retrieve and operate material is developmental and it is not until about the age of 7 yrs children develop the phonological memory skills to be able to work the contents of the phonological memory store strategically as an aid to learning. (Justice, M.E. Categorisation as a Preferred Memory Strategy. Developmental Psychology 21:1105-1110 (1985).

With regard to early literacy skills and parental involvement the Report concludes: "Whatever method is used enjoyment should be a key factor in the early stages of teaching children to read." But points out "…This can be endangered both by an overly formal approach in the early years and by a failure to teach decoding."[6] Between Memory Performance, Use of Simple Memory Strategies and Metamemory in Young Children. International Journal of Behavioural Development (1996).

"The stimuli a child experiences before the time he or she enters primary school and begins to be taught to read formally are vital to success in reading."
"Opportunities can be enhanced through pre-school programmes and the engagement of parents to provide educational development in the home."
"In this context the Government's Every Child Matters reform of children's services has a central role. (Paragraph 75)"[7]

---

[6] House of Commons: Education and Skills Committee: Teaching Children to Read: Eighth Report of Session 2004-05. Page 36, Paragraph 2.

[7] House of Commons: Education and Skills Committee; Teaching Children to Read: Eighth Report of Session 2004-05. P 37, 38, Paragraph 8.

In considering reading readiness it is worth taking a look at the non-statutory guidance material issued by The British Association for Early Childhood Education[8] which reflects the statutory framework for the Early Years Foundation Stage and gives a developmental guide chart[9] regarding both the reading and writing aspects of literacy from birth to 5+ yrs.

The Statutory Framework for the Early Years Foundation Stage which became mandatory for early years providers from 1 September 2012, (Department for Education (2012) in setting the standard for 'learning, development and care for children from birth to five' aims to provide the right foundation for each individual child by providing a range of knowledge and skills around communication and language, physical development and personal, social and emotional development, sufficient to maximise school learning opportunities. Literacy development aims to support the synthetic systematic phonics approach to reading:

"children read and understand simple sentences. They use phonic knowledge to decode regular words and read them aloud accurately. They also read some common irregular words. They demonstrate understanding when talking with others about what they have read."

With regard to writing:

"children use their phonic knowledge to write words in ways which match their spoken sounds. They also write some irregular common words. They write simple sentences which can be read by themselves and others. Some words are spelt correctly and others are phonetically plausible." (DfE. Statutory Framework for the Early Years Foundation Stage (2012) Pages 8,9).

---

[8] www.early-education.org.uk

[9] Development Matters in the Early Years Foundation Stage (EYFS) (n.d.) see also www.foundationyears.org.uk

The question of when and how to introduce children to reading has always been open to debate and no doubt always will. Various methodologies have been introduced over the years and whilst results look promising for the synthetic, systematic phonics approach to the teaching of reading, only the test of time will conclusively prove the merits of this method, one way or the other. There are many factors to be taken into account and research in the area is generally recognised to be difficult simply because of the unwieldy number of variables involved.

'Smart Read Easy' is a teaching method based on my understanding of the key areas of research into the cognitive, social and emotional development of children and most closely resembles 'the searchlights' model, since it is child-centred and has the flexibility for young children to bring the whole of their knowledge and experience to the reading process. In our society children are born into a print-driven culture and 'sight reading' or 'whole word recognition' as a result of child/adult interaction begins at an early age. This inevitability provides the foundation for reading and can be seen in the child's recognition of his/her own name.

Indeed, as we have seen, with regard to preschool children under the age of 4 yrs, their limited memory storage capacity restrains comprehension and in tests they rely on visual aid in recall. One feels wary, therefore, of driving home the synthetic phonics approach to the teaching of reading, too early, particularly as S. E. Gathercole says (*The Development of Memory* (2003)) '…there is an extremely close relationship between the children's phonological memory skills and their ability to learn new phonological material.' In my opinion to do so could be counter-productive serving as a negative reinforcer to the learning process.

In introducing the letters of the alphabet and their corresponding sounds, after a while children naturally begin to identify them when reading and in my experience this recognition becomes intrinsically motivating for they are beginning to crack the literacy code for themselves. This suggests a sufficient level of maturity has been reached to allow for the early stages of transition from using visual cues in recall to memorising from the phonological store. Gathercole says evidence indicates a linear increase in recall performance from 4 yrs to adolescence.

'The typical findings are that measures of phonological short-term memory correlate moderately with individual differences in reading ability.' (Gathercole, S.E. & Baddeley, A.D. 1993. Working Memory and Language) 'The correlations are considerably less strong than the links found between phonological memory skills and vocabulary knowledge but are nonetheless significant.'

Thus as previous research suggests, the acquisition of vocabulary is an important factor in acquiring phonological memory skills and introducing pre-school children to a number of key words plays an important part in this. Whilst various strands of research have identified a number of frequently used words which naturally overlap, many have been used and identified * thus, in the flashcard list at the end of this book. The 45 high frequency words identified by The National Literacy Strategy, which children were and are still expected to read on sight by the end of Key Stage One, are identified in the flashcard list as follows: **.

It is worth noting the DFE update for 2013: In addition to The Key Stage One reading assessment, this year the DFE have introduced the compulsory Year 1 phonics screening check which provides a short, simple screening test in fundamental phonic skills

Between the ages of 4-7yrs children are also expected to learn the following Key Stage One requirements: week days, months of the year, numbers 1-20, common colour words, name and address, name and address of school.

'Smart Read Easy' is an activity book from which each child can create a reading book for him/herself. One feels therein lies the success of the scheme, for as research shows, preschool children below the age of four rely on images to aid recall. Thus recognising the shape of a word and attaching meaning to it is the natural route into reading for young children. In being able to draw, or contribute to drawing a picture relating to the text on each story page of this book, he/she is forming an effective memory aid to text recall. As children develop, their capacity to store spoken language increases together with the ability to internally recode all non-verbal information into a phonological code, thus recall becomes more efficient to reflect the organisational structure of the phonological loop. By the age of 7, Justice, M.E. has shown learning strategies come into play (Categorization as a Preferred Memory Strategy (1985).

Although children develop at different rates, research suggests a maturation process of around three years before a child can benefit from using memory strategies to aid learning. Thus it is very important that preschool children are allowed to work at their own pace. The handling of books and learning to read should always be an enjoyable experience for preschool children and in my experience this approach to reading allows the flexibility to ensure learning to read will be a fun, exciting and rewarding experience for all concerned.

Introduction

From birth, in the majority of cultures, language and literacy are integral to a child's experience of the environment she is born into. The development of language impacts on his/her social and emotional development moving the child forward to give some degree of control over his/her environment. The pre-school stage is the optimum time for absorbing new information and it is during this rapid developmental period she is most receptive to learning. In my experience most children are advantaged in that their home environment provides a sound foundation from which new learning can flourish. Reading readiness goes hand-in-hand with the development of speech, its increasing fluency and coherence, together with an ability to listen, understand and communicate. Already parents, grandparents, nannies, family and friends have played their part in establishing reading readiness by familiarising children in their care with books and stories together with the ongoing myriad of positive interactions enabling social, emotional and cognitive development sufficient to ensure reading readiness, which, for the most part, occurs sometime between the age of two and a half to three years. In general, if your child is interested, then she is ready.

This pre-school activity book is designed to reinforce and develop children's understanding of the written word. Our environment is so filled with them it's a pretty safe bet they are already making sense of what they see around them and already understanding what some words mean.

As a qualified primary school teacher I was particularly interested in the teaching of reading and wanting to understand more, went on to gain an honours degree in psychology where my main interest centred around child development and learning. I decided to make, through play, the teaching of reading my main focus when running my own private pre-school and developed a child-centred approach which proved very successful over many years and in some quarters is still being used to great effect.

So what's the secret? It's very simple yet very effective. We ask the question, who and what is most significant in the child's life and we start from there.

So you may be a parent or grand-parent, a nanny, or a relative or friend. In whatever capacity you interact with the child you will be loved and trusted by him or her. This child, in the face of achievement of whatever kind, thrives on your praise and wants to come back for more.

You are reading this because you want to help him or her to experience the joy of learning through play, when pieces of the reading jigsaw begin to make sense because they start fitting together from what's central to his/her thinking.

In my experience various methods in the teaching of reading over the years have been purported as 'best' only to be abandoned and replaced by something else. The summarised findings of Greg Brooks, in National Foundation for Educational Research (NFER): Trends in standards of literacy in the United Kingdom, 1948-1996, conclude 'The British educational system has been generally successful in maintaining the standard of achievement in literacy.'

It is, therefore, fair to assume that for a good percentage of school children most methods employed over the years have worked but the question of what age should the teaching of reading be introduced and in particular the teaching of phonics, has always been open to debate and whilst current emphasis is on teaching to read via the synthetic phonic route it would seem there is much scepticism from many in the profession as to whether or not this is the most beneficial approach for very young children. One wonders whether more account should be taken of the findings of scientific research when the teaching of reading in schools is under consideration.

Regardless of the debate, this book, though not endorsed by the EYFS, offers an approach to the teaching of reading the author considers to be compatible with that of The Early Years Foundation Stage. It provides for the reading and understanding of simple sentences which will include common irregular words requiring sight recognition and also the decoding of regular words which the working knowledge of simple phonics will enable.

For my part, I have weighted the balance in favour of introducing teaching by whole word recognition at the same time as allowing the gentle introduction of phonics. My experience has shown, once a child has grasped the reading concept, in his/her own good time, she will recognise letters and their sounds in the words she is reading. Thus I have always erred on the side of caution with regard to the teaching of phonics to very young children and as long as there is a general level of exposure, I have found that allowing young children to forge the phonetic link for themselves facilitates understanding and learning of more complex sound structures later.

Thus this simple scheme is designed to operate on two levels. Initially you will be familiarising your child with Sam by reading and discussing the first story and encouraging him/her to colour the pictures. In the story Sam is learning to read, too. He is learning letters and their sounds from his alphabet frieze whilst also playing phonic word games on his computer which he is intent on teaching the cat. This is intended to reinforce your child's learning and understanding of the alphabet and give an understanding of phonics. It is not intended as a learning exercise, merely as a story introducing the concepts.

So this is the method. We will be encouraging a basic understanding of phonics at the same time as using whole word recognition.

To encourage recognition of the alphabet it's worth investing in a wall frieze for your child's bedroom to regularly read through the letters and their sounds in relation to the pictures. Explain that every big letter has a little friend but we only use the big capital letters at special times like writing someone's name, or the name of a place, or at the start of a line of words or for book titles.

Work through the alphabet at your child's pace following the example below. The underlined letter throughout the book is always sounded phonetically. To clarify, descending letters g j p q y are underlined as follows: g j p q y

'A says 'a' for apple'

This can be reinforced with a set of alphabet cards or various matching picture to letter games, readily available. Letter fridge magnets are also good fun for children as they allow children to play with letters and literally get the feel of them. This tactile link aids learning. For additional fun keep a sand tray letting your child's finger follow yours as you write letters in it. You can build the whole alphabet by using a glue stick to write each letter on single sheets of paper (to fit his/her work pack), then let him/her sprinkle it with sand and shake it away. He/she will love to see his/her new sand letter. Encourage him/her to follow the shape with his/her finger to allow his/her sense of touch to aid his/her learning. Later you can progress to writing whole words in this way thereby building a useful collection of his/her chosen words to work through.

During the recognition process of 'whole' words, the child internalises the word's pattern or shape, like a picture. This is reinforced by his contribution to the meaning of the word in his/her drawing of it.

Thus:

Orange Pip

Added reinforcement is achieved by showing him/her the flashcard of the word and asking him/her to read it out and then match it to the same word on the page. When he/she progresses to linking words and making sentences, encourage him/her to build these with the flashcards matching the words on the page for him/herself.

Read the Guide Page before commencing the session. Initially these are repetitious for quick reference. The sessions should be brief and fun. Remember to date each page worked and in the 'Notes' section at the end of the book add any words you would like to give extra revision to, to aid your child's learning.

At the start of each session encourage him/her to read the flashcards, then go back to the beginning of the book, and placing his/her index finger under each word against the page, encourage him/her to read the word(s) on each page allowing him/her to turn the pages for him/herself. You will be making flashcards to personalise the scheme, particularly in the early stages where family names, pet names, favourite toys etc. make the project meaningful and fun.

It cannot be emphasised enough that your praise is the key factor in the achievement of reading goals. There should always be a residual level of praise but initially, liberally praise any interest shown and as the process gets underway this can be gradually reduced and returned in fuller measure each time progress is made. Not only will she enjoy your verbal praise, but also she will be excited as you tick his/her work, explaining that special word 'Excellent' as you write it and follow it by adding a star.

By creating this first reading book you will be laying a sound foundation for your child's reading development now, and for the future you will be building a precious record of reading achievement of which you both can be justly proud. Work for just five to ten minutes, here and there, a couple of times a week, when it suits you both. I have found working with young children in this way provides a sure return on time invested. The method is informal and flexible. It is up to you how you choose to work this book. Every child's progress rate is different, thus the phonetic content overlaps into Key Stage 1. As your child moves forward to the second stage of this book, by encouraging the recognition and use of phonics as an aid to deciphering whole words, you will be helping to develop his/her analytical skills which will become a valuable aid in further developing his/her reading skills in the future.

By working through the book you will have introduced your child to most of the key words required for learning to read. The word list is compiled from the suggested learning activity pages and the most frequently used words are identified thus: *, and ** (to indicate the 45 high frequency words The National Literacy Strategy identifies as needed to learn to read). Inevitably there is considerable overlap from differing sources with regard to the compilation of such a list but the key words used here are the most cited, and even the recognition of relatively few, have, in my experience enabled young children in my care to progress their reading skills with confidence and enthusiasm. The word list is provided for your use and is not intended to be an achievement target, per se.

We used this scheme very successfully for eighteen years in my own private pre-school and only ever had positive feedback as to the head start it gave the children, enabling an easy transition from nursery to school.

The second part of this activity book is a progression of the first, further introducing new words and presenting opportunities for the recognition and understanding of phonic blending whilst the story of 'Sam' unfolds.

With regard to the gender issue I have tried to be even-handed and when possible have used 'she' for readers to extract from appropriately. However, in order that it does not become a distraction, guide pages will alternate using a single reference to either boy or girl.

Now begin by simply reading the story of Sam to your child and asking if she would like to colour the pictures.

Sam

Sam is four. He can't wait to be five because he wants a big red ball for his birthday. He sees it in the shop window every morning on his way to nursery. It has two eyes, one nose and one mouth.

The toy shop

'This is the shop, here. I want that,' he says to Mummy. 'I want that big red ball now. Look, it is smiling at me, Mummy. Can I have it now?'

'No Sam no, not just now, you'll have to wait until your birthday, but you'll only get it if you are good.'

'But I am being good,' says Sam.

'Not yesterday,' says Mummy. 'Yesterday you pulled the cat's tail, then chased him out of the garden. He won't want to come home if you keep doing that.'

'But I was only playing with him Mummy.'

'That's not playing,' says Mummy, 'you could have hurt him. Daddy was very cross with you, too.'

'Sorry Mummy,' Sam says. 'I will be good if I can have that big red ball for my birthday.'

Sam looks at all the things in the window. He sees a picture of a big red ball.

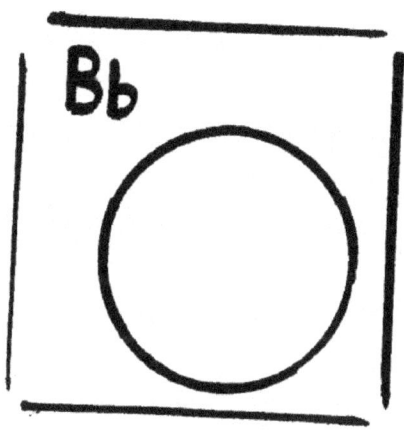

The big red ball

'Mummy I want that. I want that big red ball now.'

'First of all you should remember to say "please" Sam,' Mummy says.

'Please Mummy, please can I have that now?'

Mummy takes Sam into the shop. Sam watches the man unfold all the pictures to show him the alphabet frieze.

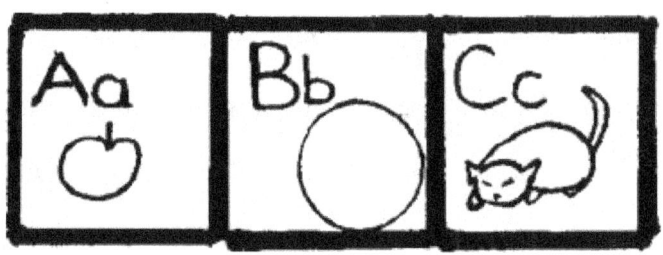

The alphabet frieze

'I like this Mummy,' says Sam. We have this one in the nursery. Please can I have it now?'

'Yes, of course you can Sam. We'll put it on your bedroom wall, then you will see the picture of the big red ball and it will remind you to be a good boy.'

'Thank you Mummy,' says Sam. He gives Mummy a big kiss. 'I love you Mummy,' he says.

'I love you, too,' says Mummy.

'Can we put it on the wall when we get home?' asks Sam.

'As long as you are a good boy at nursery,' says Mummy.

Sam forgets all about being a good boy at nursery, he is too excited for that. He can't wait to go home to see his new alphabet frieze on his bedroom wall.

Sam in the sand

Sam is very naughty. He throws the sand at all the children.

He looks at the picture of the big red ball on the alphabet frieze but he forgets to be good.

Sam in the water

He pulls the plug from the water table to let the water flood all over the floor.

He looks at the picture of the big red ball on the alphabet frieze but he forgets to be good.

Sam is messy

He breaks his biscuits into little bits and drops them into his milk.

He looks at the picture of the big red ball on the alphabet frieze but he forgets to be good.

He splashes the teacher's face with red paint and tips the blue paint all over her shoes.

Sam splashes the teacher

He looks at the picture of the big red ball on the alphabet frieze but he forgets to be good.

He spills the glue and spreads it around the floor with his hands to make everyone's shoes sticky.

Sam spills the glue

He looks at the picture of the big red ball on the alphabet frieze but he forgets to be good.

When it is home time he throws all the children's coats on the floor and tosses their hats in the air.

Sam throws the coats

He looks at the picture of the big red ball on the alphabet frieze. Sam knows he forgot to be good.

He looks at the coats on the floor of the cloakroom.
Sam knows he forgot to be good.

He looks at the sand all over the floor.
Sam knows he forgot to be good.

He looks at the water all over the floor.
Sam knows he forgot to be good.

He looks at the footprints in the white glue on the floor.
Sam knows he forgot to be good.

He looks down to his teacher's shoes covered in blue paint.
Sam knows he forgot to be good.

He looks up to her face splashed with red paint. She is very cross.
Sam knows he forgot to be good.
'Just take him home,' she says to his Mummy.

'I'm sorry Mummy,' says Sam on the way home. 'I forgot to be good. I want that picture on my wall. I want to see the big red ball on my wall.'

'We'll see about that,' says Mummy. 'We'll see about that.'

Sam eats all his dinner.

'I think it would be a good idea for you to calm down and spend some quiet time in your bedroom this afternoon,' says Mummy.

Mummy goes upstairs with Sam. Sam opens the bedroom door and on the wall he sees his new alphabet frieze. He points to the letters, Bb

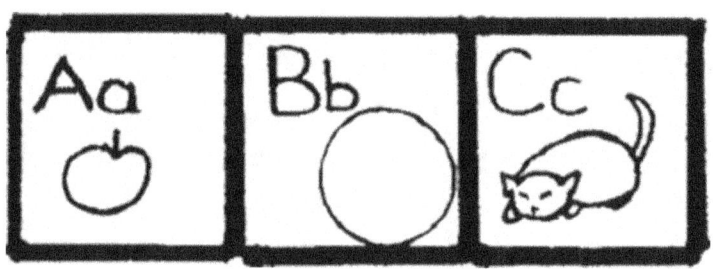

Sam's alphabet frieze

'Look Mummy, that's the big red ball,' says Sam. He is happy now.

'That's right Sam,' says Mummy. 'The letter B says <u>b</u> for <u>b</u>all.'

'B says <u>b</u> for <u>b</u>all,' Sam says, 'and I am getting a big red ball for my birthday.'

'Yes you are Sam but only if you are a good boy.'

'I forgot to be good today,' says Sam, 'but I will be good tomorrow.'

Mummy gives Sam a big hug. She says, 'It's hard to be good all the time but as long as you try to be a good boy Sam you will get that big red ball for your birthday.'

Sam is very happy. He likes his new alphabet frieze.

'Let's say all the letters Mummy.' says Sam. 'A says a for apple. E says e for egg. O says o for orange.'

Mummy is surprised. 'You are a clever boy Sam,' she says.

'We say these at nursery,' he says. 'I know all of these.'

Mummy is very surprised. 'We can make words from these sounds,' she says. She gets a pen and some paper to write them down.

'Now Sam show me the letter Cc.'

'Good boy, now what does that say?'

'C says c for cat.'

'Clever boy Sam. Let's write it down. Now show me the letter Aa. What does that say?'

'A says a for apple.'

'Very good Sam. Mummy writes it down.

'Now show me the letter Tt. What does that say?

'T says t̲ for t̲ent,' says Sam.

'Well done Sam,' says Mummy. She writes it down.

'Now Sam,' says Mummy. 'Do you remember who you have to be kind to?'

'I know, I know,' says Sam. He sounds the letters,

<u>c a t</u>

It's the cat Mummy, it's the cat.'

Mummy hugs him. 'You are such a clever boy Sam,' she says.

'I will be good and I will let the cat play with my new red ball,' he says, giving Mummy a big hug and kiss.

Guide:

Talk about the story then read the storyline at the bottom of the next page. Draw a picture together of Mummy and Sam.

Sam loves Mummy

Guide:

Talk about the story, then read the storyline at the bottom of the next page. Draw a picture together of Daddy and Sam.

Sam loves Daddy

Guide:

Talk about the story, then read the storylines at the bottom of the next page. Draw a picture together of Sam and Orange Pip. Tell your child how much Sam loves the alphabet and later in the book he'll see Sam trying to teach the cat to read.

Now talk about Sam's alphabet frieze and how Sam is learning the names and sounds of all the letters. Tell him inside this book is an alphabet book with pictures for him to colour.

Sam likes the cat. His name is Orange Pip.

Aa Bb Cc Dd Ee Ff Gg Hh Ii Jj Kk Ll
Mm Nn Oo Pp Qq Rr Ss Tt Uu Vv
Ww Xx Yy Zz

My Alphabet Book

----

abcdefghijklmnopqrstuvwxyz
ABCDEFGHIJKLMNOPQRSTUVWXYZ

Aa

A says <u>a</u> for apple

Bb

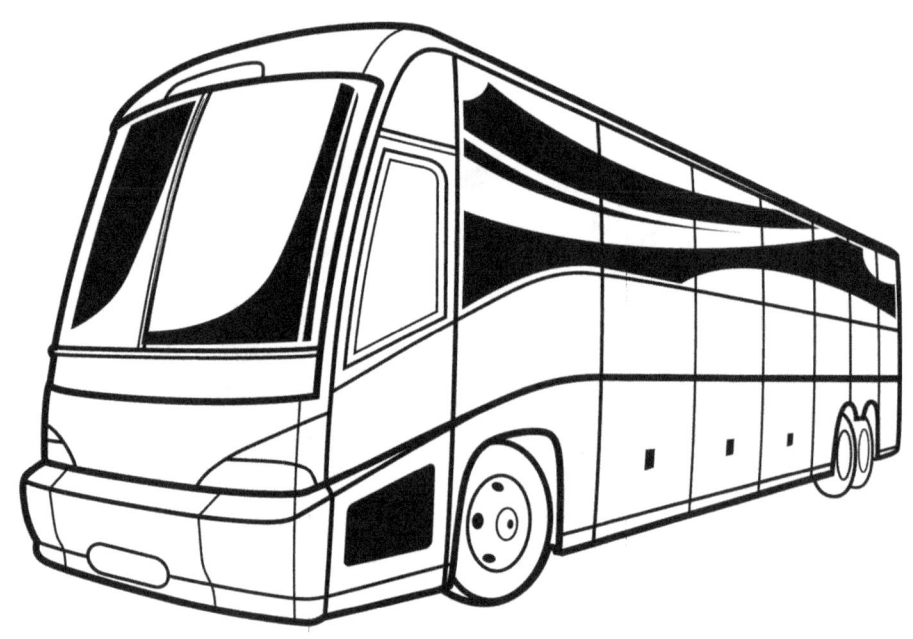

B says <u>b</u> for
bus

Cc

C says c̲ for
cat

Dd

D says <u>d</u> for
doll

Ee

E says e for egg

Ff

F says f for fish

Gg

G says g for
gull

Hh

H says <u>h</u> for
hat

Ii

I says i for
imp

Jj

J says j for
jam

Kk

K says k for kitten

Ll

L says l for
lemon

Mm

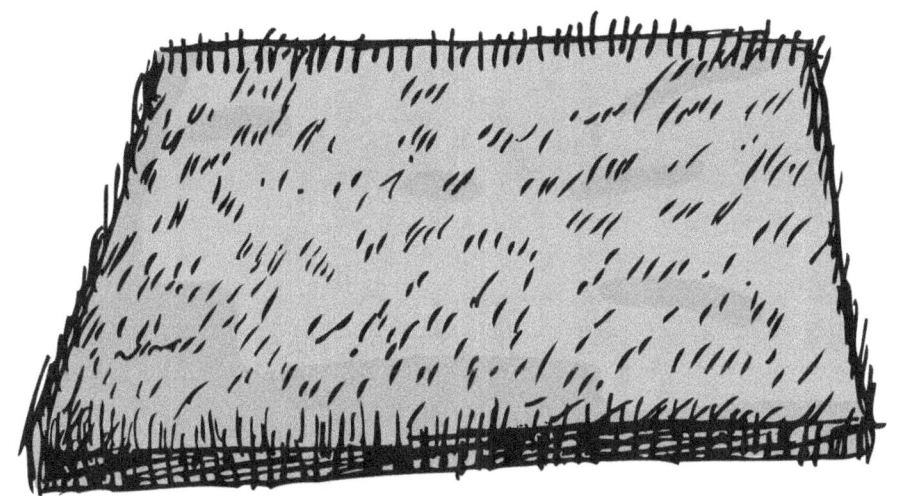

M says <u>m</u> for
mat

Nn

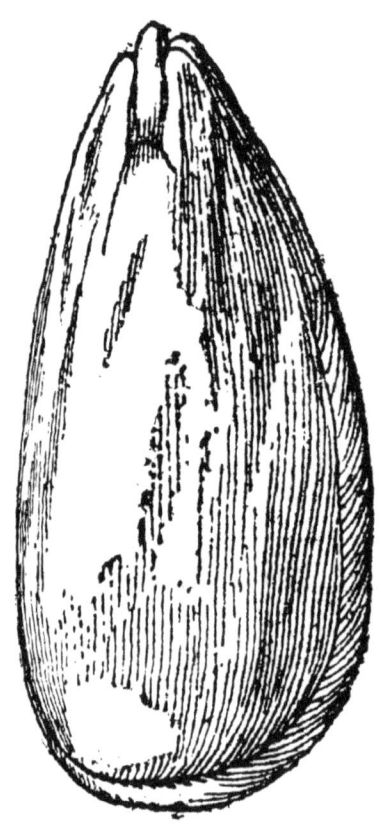

N says <u>n</u> for nut

Oo

O says o for orange

Pp

P says p for
pot

Qq

Q says q for queen

Rr

R says r for rabbit

Ss

S says s̲ for sun

Tt

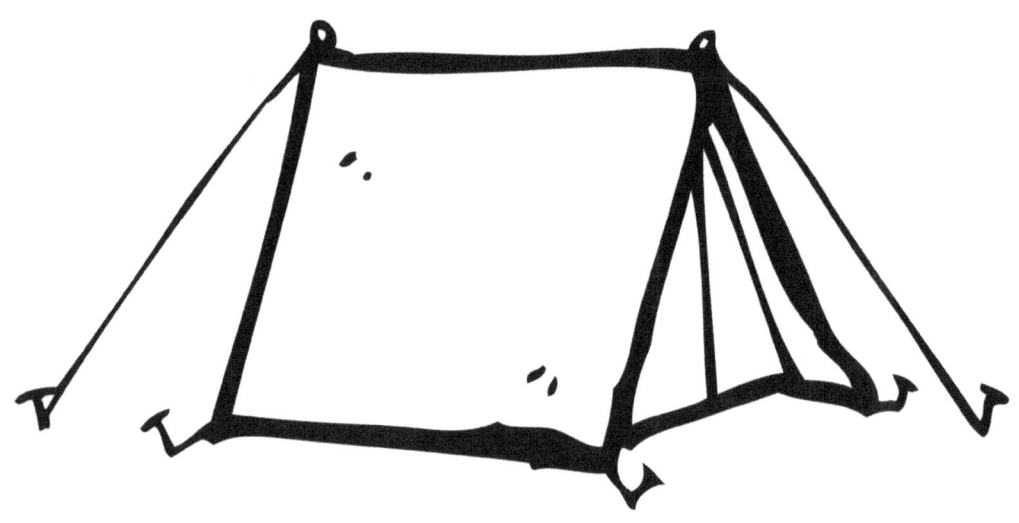

T says t for tent

Uu

U says <u>u</u> for umbrella

Vv

V says v for
van

Ww

W says w for wellingtons

Xx

X says x for
x-ray

Yy

Y says y for
yacht

Zz

Z says z for zebra

Getting Started

Materials required in addition to this book:

Adult
scissors for cutting out flashcards
plain card/paper for making flashcards
broad black felt-tip pen
reward stickers (or draw your own star), pen
firm support for left hand working pages of this book

Child
pencil
coloured crayons / felt-tips
envelope for flash-cards
alphabet frieze or cards
clear plastic zip bag (they love to see into their work pack)
practice exercise book for any additional reinforcement

Method

Session 1
1. On the title page under the heading 'My Reading Book' write the child's full name eg.

Andrew Roberts

Encourage him to say this at each sitting to engender recognition. Make a same name flashcard and encourage him to read and match them. Write his name on the first work page and encourage him to draw a picture. Ask him to match his name flashcard to his name written on the page.

2. Ask your child who or what he would like to put next in the book, saying, 'We'll make a name card, shall we?' In doing this you are establishing who or what is most significant to him at this particular time. It may be a favourite TV or computer game character, or a particular toy or pet. He may wish to begin with Mummy or Daddy, or siblings, pets, other non-resident relatives or special friends but never suggest these. The success of this scheme depends upon your child driving it.

Make flashcards to personalise this stage.

Always let the child guide you as to which name to introduce next.
Let's assume the new pet dog Max takes precedence over everything else and we start with 'Max', use the blanks at the end of the book to make a flashcard and with a black felt-tip pen, let your child watch you write the word eg.

Max

Encourage her to talk about 'Max' whilst holding the flashcard at the same time as you write the word at the bottom of the first blank page in the book.

3. Either one or both of you, draw a picture of 'Max' and ask your child to colour it in.

4. Praise the drawing and ask your child to tell you who it is, from the picture, from the flashcard and from the name under the picture.

5. Whatever the response praise liberally, tick and reinforce with a written note eg.

Good work Anna *

This can be reinforced with a sticker or draw your own star.

6. Write the date on the page and as you progress note any words that need reinforcing in the 'Notes' section at the end of the book.

7. Let your child return all items to her own bag and agree on a place to keep it.

Following Sessions

Be guided by your child as to when the next session should take place. In all probability your child will arrive with her work pack of her own accord. Remember, the work up to the Second Series is designed to cover a minimum period of two years. During this time encourage your child to read widely with you. She will be delighted when familiar words are recognised in story books.

All children are different, over time, some may wish to progress further with this activity book, others may not. If interest is shown and progress is made and your child is happy to attempt the second stage, encourage her to read the next story in exactly the same way, reinforcing new words as before. As the stories begin to introduce a greater phonic awareness, encourage the use of this to help your child learn new words arising appropriate to the level of introduction.

Remember this is an activity book intended to be fun and she may simply wish to draw and colour as you read the second set of stories.

With regard to the final story, 'Billy Ball', depending on your child's interest and progress, using your own exercise book for working you may like to break this story down into short sentences for her to read. Focus on the NLS 45 key words as they arise and new words that lend themselves to phonetic analysis within the phonic structures introduced here.

We are aiming to familiarise your child with the joys of reading and this can only be achieved without pressure. It is not expected that she learns all the words introduced in the whole series of books before she starts school. Each book contains frequently used words essential for learning to read and the first series in itself will provide a considerable foundation for the pre-school child. It doesn't matter whether you work with her every day or once a week, as long as you are both happy to enjoy another short session together which is likely to be fun, as long as she is the decision maker in the learning process.

At the start of each session encourage him to go through all his flashcards then ask him to read each page of his book from the beginning. Praise liberally, taking care to repeat your delight at his progress on every page by repeating your written message of praise.

Follow the scheme as it is presented in the book. The stories are designed to gradually introduce common verbs and nouns to enable simple sentence construction. This is an activity book which progresses through easily understood personal and social concepts. The final story 'Billy Ball' broadens to include basic mathematical language set in a context meaningful to the child.

Adult instructions appear in italics alongside each blank work page. To summarise, maximum benefit will be achieved by working with your child at each session in the following way.

1) Revise the alphabet.
2) Revise flashcards.
3) Match flashcards to each worked page.
4) Initially ask your child to read his work from the beginning of the book each time until the word(s) on each page are known and read with confidence.
5) Discuss and introduce the next word. Write it in his book and ask him to draw a picture. Help your child along. Once he has added his own contribution, eg. eyes, mouth, ears, hair, arms, legs, or simply touched it with a crayon, between you, you have made it his.

Please note: the same word introduced with both a small and a capital letter is treated as two separate words for the purpose of this book. Words included in the NLS 45 key word list, appearing in this book in both these forms, are listed to reflect this. I have added the words 'Mummy' and 'Daddy' to this list, since their use generally precedes that of 'Mum' and 'Dad'.

Guide:

Explain that this is the start of the book and as your child will be making it, help her to understand by saying, 'We will need to write your name so everyone will know what a clever girl you are.'

From the alphabet section find the first letter of her name, pointing to the capital letter and remind her how the big capital letter is very important and used at the start of names as well as the start of reading lines, pointing them out in the previous story.

Make a name card and write her name in the space provided.

Before moving on ask her to read the card and match it to her name on the front page.

Now write her name on the first page of the work book and help her to draw a picture of herself. Again match the name card to the name you have just written, then encourage your child to do the same.

Praise liberally and add a positive comment to the work before ending the session.

My Reading Book

Examples of worked pages:

Andrew Roberts

Max

Guide:

Begin the session by working through the alphabet.

Together read through the letters of the alphabet by naming each letter and then repeat this phonetically by reading **'A says a for apple'**, *etc.*

To help him later, try to keep the pronunciation of letters short and sharp so the sounds will blend more easily to form a word eg. **mur, aar, tu,** *will not readily blend to read* **mat**, *as a short, sharp pronunciation* **m a t** *will.*

Ask your child to read his name card and match it to his name on the previous title page and then match it to his name on the first page in the workbook by placing the card of top. Encourage him to cover and remove the name card, repeating his name each time.

Now ask who he would like to add next to his new book. Then tell him that we need another name card. Let's assume he's excited about the new dog and it's called 'Max'. Say, 'Let's make a card for Max, then.'

Hold it up and ask him 'Whose card is this?' Then say to him 'Let's draw a picture of Max, shall we?'

Follow this with 'Who have we drawn?' Then, 'Let's write 'Max' below it.'

Help him along and praise his work as previously described.

Guide:

Begin the session by working through the alphabet.

Together read through the letters of the alphabet by naming each letter and then repeat this phonetically by reading **'B says b for bus'**, *etc. To help her later, try to keep the pronunciation of letters short and sharp so the sounds will blend more easily to form a word eg.* **mur, aar, tu,** *will not readily blend to read* **mat,** *as a short, sharp pronunciation* **m a t** *will.*

At the start of this session encourage your child to read the flashcards, then go back to the beginning of the book, encouraging her to read her name matching it to her name on the title page, before reading and matching the word on the next page; allowing her to turn the page for herself. Give liberal praise and practice until a correct match of each name card to name is achieved.

Reminding her that we always use the big, important, capital letter for names, point to the capital letter at the start of the name, eg. **M**ax *Return to the alphabet saying* **'Now let's see if we can find M for Max'** *sounding out the* **M** *phonetically. Encourage your child to repeat with you,* **'M for Max'**. *Ask her to point to the letter* **M** *in the alphabet and then point to the letter* **M** *on the flashcard. Ask her to read the flashcard again. In doing this we are presenting the opportunity for phonic recognition of letters in words that are meaningful to her.*

Use your blank flashcards to personalise the scheme, particularly as you progress in this early stage where family names, names of friends and pet names can make the project meaningful and fun.

Now ask who she would like to put next in her new book. Then tell her that we need a name card as you cut out a flashcard or a blank to make one. Let's assume it's **'Teddy'**.

Hold it up and ask her 'Whose card is this?' Then say to her 'Let's draw a picture of Teddy, shall we?' Follow this with 'Who have we drawn?' Then, 'Let's write **'Teddy'** *below it.' Help her along and praise her work as previously described.*

Guide:

Begin the session by working through the alphabet.

Together read through the letters of the alphabet by naming each letter and then repeat this phonetically by reading **'C says c for cat'**, *etc. To help him later, try to keep the pronunciation of letters short and sharp so the sounds will blend more easily to form a word eg.* **mur, aar, tu,** *will not readily blend to read* **mat,** *as a short, sharp pronunciation* **m a t** *will.*

At the start of this session encourage your child to read the flashcards, then go back to the beginning of the book, encouraging him to read his name matching it to his name on the title page, before reading and matching the word on the next page; allowing him to turn the page for himself. Give liberal praise and practice until a correct match of each name card to name is achieved. Reminding him that we always use the big, important, capital letter for names, point to the capital letter at the start of the name, eg. **T**eddy *Return to the alphabet saying* **'Now let's see if we can find T for Teddy'** *sounding out the* **T** *phonetically. Encourage your child to repeat with you,* **'T for Teddy'**. *Ask your child to point at the letter* **T** *in the alphabet and then point to the letter* **T** *on the flashcard. Ask him to read the flashcard again. In doing this we are presenting the opportunity for phonic recognition of letters in words that are meaningful to him.*

 Use the blank flashcards to personalise the scheme, particularly as you progress in this early stage where names of toys, family names, names of friends and pet names can make the project meaningful and fun.

Guide:

At the start of every session revise the alphabet, then encourage your child to read the flashcards, then go back to the beginning of the book, encouraging her to read her name matching it to her name on the title page, before reading and matching the word on the next page; allowing her to turn the pages for herself. Give liberal praise and practice until a correct match of card to name is achieved.

*Now ask who she would like to put next in her new book. Then tell her that we need a name card as you cut out a flashcard or a blank to make one. Let's assume it's '***Sam***'. Hold it up and ask her 'Whose card is this?' Then say to her 'Let's draw a picture of Sam, shall we?' Follow this with 'Who have we drawn?' Then, 'Let's write ***Sam***' below it.' Help her along and praise her work as previously described.*

*Reminding her that we always use the big, important, capital letter for names, point to the capital letter at the start of each name, going through them one at a time eg. **S**am Return to the alphabet saying 'Now let's see if we can find* **S** *for* **Sam** *sounding out the* **S** *phonetically. Encourage the child to repeat with you, '***S** *for* **Sam**'. *Ask your child to point at the letter* **S** *in the alphabet and then point to the letter* **S** *in* **Sam** *on the flashcard. Ask her to read the flashcard again. In doing this we are presenting the opportunity for phonic recognition of letters in words that are meaningful to her.*

As new words are introduced and working with names beginning with a single sound only continue to match the first letter to the alphabet phonetically in exactly the same way as before, eg. **Sam** *begins with a single sound* **S**.

At this point continue to personalise the scheme, moving on to make flashcards. Ask who or what she would like to write next. Let's assume it's her sister 'Lucy'. Write the name on the card and ask her 'Whose card is this?' Followed by 'Let's draw a picture of Lucy, shall we?' Titles, eg. Aunty, should be written on a separate flashcard. Continue in exactly the same way, following the same procedure for each session, working through all her chosen names, one per session. Try to contain the number of names to around six.

57

Guide:

Follow the same procedure. Remind him that we always use the big, important, capital letter for names. Point to the capital letter at the start of each name, including his own, going through them one at a time eg. **<u>A</u>ndrew** *Return to the alphabet saying* **'Now let's see if we can find <u>A</u> for Andrew'** *sounding out the* **A** *phonetically. Encourage your child to repeat with you,* **'<u>A</u> for Andrew'**. *Ask your child to point to the letter* **A** *in the alphabet and then point to the letter* **A** *on the flashcard. Ask him to read the flashcard again. As new words are introduced continue to match the first letter to the alphabet phonetically in exactly the same way as before. If the word does not start with a capital letter then point this out explaining that it is not a name or the first word at the start of a line. Explain any anomalies that may arise as new words are introduced, eg.* **I**, *saying* **'I** *can be used on its own when it says its own name to become a word.*

When confident your child can read all his chosen names in the book and can identify the initial letter and its sound, move on using flashcards to introduce two new words, **I** *and* **love**. *Introduce them together then ask your child to find his name card. Then with the flashcards build the sentence. Eg.* **I love Andrew Roberts** *Ask him to repeat the words after you. Then ask him to give you the card that says* **I** *then the card that says* **love** *then the card that says* **Andrew Roberts**. *With his help build the sentence again, read it together and then ask him to read it by himself. Repeat the card game, changing the order around. Write the sentence at the bottom of the page and ask him to draw a picture of himself, helping him if he needs it. The Following session revise the activity and when your child is ready suggest you play a new game by asking whose name did he want at the very start of the book. Turn back to that page for him to read the name and find it from the flashcards. Let's assume it's* **Max**. *Arrange the flashcards on the table to read* **I love Max** *helping your child read the sentence, pointing to each word as you say them. Repeat this three or four times, then write the sentence at the bottom of the page saying each word as you do so. Read the sentence to your child then ask him to read it to you. Suggest drawing a picture of himself with Max. Praise liberally your child's attempt however minimal the contribution. Now read the line together and then ask him to say it on his own. Match the flashcards to the words then ask him which word is first. Ask him to place it on the table and then follow with the next one and finally the last. Ask him to read the sentence he has made again from the cards and then from the book. Again praise liberally as you tick and write an encouraging word.*

Example of worked page:

I love Max

Guide page:

Keep practicing in exactly the same way, matching the first letter of each word to the alphabet, saying the letter and the sound. Continue revising by reading and matching all flashcard names to the pages and when confident your child can read them all including **I** *and* **love** *move on to the next name.*

From the flashcards ask your child to give you the card that says **I** *, then the card that says* **love.** *Place them in order on the table and ask her to place the* **Max** *card at the end. Ask her to read the sentence and then ask her whose card he would like to work with next. Ask her to take the* **Max** *card away and replace it with her chosen one. Let's assume it's* **Lucy***. Ask her to read the sentence she has just made.*

I love Lucy

Help your child by reading the sentence together, pointing to each word as you say them. Repeat this three or four times, then write the sentence at the bottom of the page saying each word as you do so. Read the sentence to your child then ask her to read it to you. Suggest she draws a picture of herself and Lucy. Praise liberally your child's attempt however minimal the contribution. Now read the line together and then ask her to say it on her own. Match the flashcards to the words then ask her which word is first. Ask her to place it on the table and then follow with the next one and finally the last. Ask her to read the sentence she has made again from the cards and then from the book. Again praise liberally as you tick and write an encouraging word. Draw a star or stick one on. As she progresses let her draw or stick her own star on as a reward.

Guide:

Begin with the alphabet following the same procedure as for each session.

Continue to work through all the names your child has chosen in exactly the same way, working one page at a time. At the end of each session place all the cards on the table and ask him to give you the card that says, eg. **Max, Lucy, I, Teddy, love, Aunty,** *etc. Do this in whatever order you choose, mixing them to ensure he is recognising each one. Reinforce as described in the previous session.*

Guide:

Keep practicing in exactly the same way, matching the first letter of each word to the alphabet, saying the letter and the phoneme (sound). Continue revising by reading and matching all flashcard names to the pages and when confident your child can read them all including **I** *and* **love** *introduce the new word* **and** *working it with her chosen names as before eg.*

Andrew and Max

Remove one name asking her to find her own name card to go with **Lucy** *instead, eg.*

Lucy and Anna Roberts

Cover **Roberts** *with a blank flashcard explaining how at home and with people we know well we usually use our first names. Remove the blank card and suggest making a new flashcard of her first name only to add to the others. Now read it out together.* **Lucy and Anna**

Continue by asking her to choose a different name selected from her flashcards, eg. **Teddy** *working all the different names in different combinations with the new word* **and** *eg.*

Lucy and Teddy   Max and Anna   Sam and Aunty Wendy

Encourage her to read each combination of words after she has made it. Now ask her which one she would like to write in her book. Let her select the cards helping her with the order of the words. Ask her to read the line and draw a picture. Give liberal praise for her efforts. From the flashcards ask your child to give you the card that says **Aunty** *, then the card that says* **and** *next the card that says* **Wendy** *finally the card that says* **Sam***.*

Continue in exactly the same way working different names in conjunction with **and** *until she knows the word and the letter and the phonetic sound of* **A***. Let your child be the guide as to which combinations of names she wants, working just one set at each session. Continue to match, write and read as before, giving liberal praise.*

Example of flashcard structures:

word structures

Guide:

Start the session as before, working through the alphabet, where appropriate revising and matching letters and sounds, working through flashcards and reading each page of the book, praising your child's achievements.

Introduce two new words **This** *and* **is** *in exactly the same way as before, working through a different name each session, until you are confident your child knows the words, eg.*

This is Max

This is Teddy

This is Lucy

This is Aunty Wendy

87

Guide:

Continue revising and reinforcing as before. Introduce the new word **Here** *and* **here** *in both forms. Work this with the existing flashcards to build different sentences eg.*

Sam is here

Max is here

Here is Lucy

Teddy is here

Here is Aunty Wendy

Continue to create pages as before working one sentence each page, allowing your child to draw and colour to represent the sentence as he sees fit. Read and match with flashcards reinforcing his achievement with liberal praise.

Guide:

Continue revising and reinforcing as before. Introduce one new word **good**. *Work this with the existing flashcards to build different sentences eg.*

Max is good.

Andrew is good.

Lucy is good.

Continue to create pages as before working one sentence each page, allowing your child to draw and colour to represent the sentence as she sees fit. Read and match with flashcards reinforcing her achievement with liberal praise.

Guide:

Continue revising and reinforcing as before. Introduce one new word **How**. *Work this with the existing flashcards to build different sentences eg.*

How is Max.

How is Sam.

How is Lucy.

Continue to create pages as before working one sentence each page, allowing your child to draw and colour to represent the sentence as he sees fit. Read and match with flashcards reinforcing his achievement with liberal praise.

Guide:

Continue revising and reinforcing as before, matching, saying and sounding initial letters as appropriate. Working with all the flashcards and making duplicates if necessary, build different sentences, eg:

This is Teddy.

How is Teddy.

Teddy is good.

I love Max and I love Teddy

Lucy is here and Andrew is here.

Continue to create pages as before working one sentence each page, allowing your child to choose, draw and colour each sentence, representing the sentence as she sees fit. Read and match with flashcards reinforcing her achievement with liberal praise.

Guide:

Continue revising and reinforcing as before, continuing to match, say and sound initial letters as appropriate, sentence building with flashcards and reading all the pages in his book. Revise these sentences from his book, eg: **How is Teddy***, etc. Write this in his book and follow with the answer.*

How is Teddy. Teddy is good.

Ask him to read it to you and draw a picture. Ask him to read it again and then match the flashcards to the words.

Continue to create pages as before working one sentence each page, by working through the combinations, one page per session until he knows all words and is able to say and sound the first letter of each where appropriate.

Allow him to draw and colour to represent the sentence as he sees fit. Read and match with flashcards reinforcing his achievement with liberal praise.

How is Max. Max is good.

How is Lucy. Lucy is good.

Please remember these are examples only. You and your child will be working with his/her chosen word names.

Guide:

Continue revising and reinforcing as before. Introduce the new words **Does, like** *and* **eggs** *using flashcards and sentence build working this in conjunction with all family names to build different sentences eg.*

Does Teddy like eggs.

Does Max like eggs.

Does Lucy like eggs.

Continue to create pages as before working one sentence each page, allowing your child to draw and colour to represent the sentence as she sees fit. Read and match with flashcards reinforcing her achievement with liberal praise.

Guide:
Continue revising and reinforcing as before. Introduce the new word **oranges** *using flashcards to sentence build working this in conjunction with all family names to build different sentences eg.*

Does Teddy like oranges.

Does Max like oranges.

Does Lucy like oranges.

Continue to create pages as before working one sentence each page, allowing your child to draw and colour to represent the sentence as he sees fit. Read and match with flashcards reinforcing his achievement with liberal praise.

Guide page

Continue revising and reinforcing as before. Introduce two new words **Do,** *and* **you** *using flashcards build the sentence*

Do you like eggs.

Write the sentence in her book and ask her to match the flashcards with the words then read it together allowing your child to draw and colour to represent the sentence as she sees fit. Finally read and match the flashcards reinforcing her achievement with liberal praise.

Guide:

Continue revising and reinforcing as before. Introduce two new words **Yes** *and* **No** *using the following flashcards build each of the following sentences.*

Do you like eggs. Yes.

Do you like eggs. No.

Ask him which is correct. Write the sentence in his book and ask him to match the flashcards with the words then read it together allowing your child to draw and colour to represent the sentence as he sees fit. Finally read and match the flashcards reinforcing his achievement with liberal praise.

Guide:

Continue revising and reinforcing as before. Reinforcing the two new words **Yes** *and* **No** *by rearranging the flashcards to build each of the following sentences allowing her to answer the question with the correct flashcard, eg:*

Do you like eggs. No

Do you like oranges. Yes

Does Max like eggs. No

Does Teddy like oranges. Yes

Ask her which sentence she would like next. Write it in her book and ask her to match the flashcards with the words then read it together allowing your child to draw and colour to represent the sentence as she sees fit. Finally read and match the flashcards reinforcing her achievement with liberal praise.

Guide:

Continue revising and reinforcing as before. Working with flashcard word names and one entry per session, use the next few sessions to reinforce the following recently introduced words: **Does, Do, you, like, eggs, oranges**, **Yes** *and* **No** *by rearranging the flashcards to build each of the suggested sentences allowing your child to answer* **Yes** *or* **No** *to the question with the correct flashcard.*

Do you like eggs.

Do you like oranges.

Does Max like eggs.

Does Teddy like oranges.

Ask him which sentence he would like you to write next in his book and ask him to match the flashcards with the words then read it together allowing him to draw and colour to represent the sentence as he sees fit. Finally read and match the flashcards reinforcing his achievement with liberal praise.

What's next?

Having progressed and consolidated his/her reading skills at your child's own pace you are both to be congratulated on creating his/her very first book. You have achieved this together without pressure, because you have only worked with him/her at his/her request or received a positive response at your suggestion to read, working only when you have both been happy to do so. The key factor here is allowing the process to remain child-centred to maximise enjoyment. This facilitates easy progress since, in my experience, it has always proved to be fun and rewarding.

Remember you are only *introducing* him/her to reading and as previously explained this scheme can be worked at any pace you both enjoy. There is no hurry! It is certainly not envisaged pre-school children will be able to read all the key words noted in this book prior to school entry. Rather the latter part of this book may be returned to again and again as an aid to learning and reinforcing his/her reading development. It's up to your child and you, of course, to take what you wish from it. If your child is happy and enjoying the experience then continue. Before doing so, however, it's worth revising the alphabet, ticking off the names and sounds of all the letters he/she knows. This will give you guidance for further reinforcement if necessary.

The 45 NLS key words are introduced gradually in the following 15 stories and identified thus **. In helping your child with the reading of each of these stories, it is worth giving additional reinforcement to these words for although children will not be required to know them all until the end of Key Stage One, focussing on them during the course of working through this book will certainly help in the achievement of this. They will also be expected to bring to school a knowledge of short vowel sounds together with initial and final sounds in words, so it is worth spending some time on this, working within the phonic framework introduced here.

When your child shows interest, encourage the deployment of phonic skills in the learning of new words. Help your child by writing the letters down as you hear him/her making the sounds, then blend the sounds to make the word. Using your pen allow him/her to trace over your letters, ensuring the correct pen hold and guiding him/her to achieve the correct letter formation.

Please remember, however, this book goes well beyond foundation level and again I emphasise it should always be worked at your child's own pace. Use it to suit the needs of your child and consider enjoyment the priority as she reads, writes, draws and colours, to make this book his/her own.

Summing up

At this stage, in addition to learning word names she has chosen, she has been introduced to the phonic alphabet and worked with words beginning with the short vowel sounds of

<u>a</u> <u>e</u> <u>i</u> <u>o</u>

(<u>u</u> is introduced in new word 'up' Book 6 P8)

Your child has also been introduced to these words, 8 of which are key to the NLS marked thus** :

**and, Do, Does, good, eggs, Here, here, How, **I, **is, **like, love, **No,

oranges, **This, **this, **Yes, **you

The next section will continue to build on these words in the same way as before by reinforcing whole word recognition with the use of flashcards, at the same time as encouraging him/her to apply his/her knowledge of vowel and consonant sounds by sounding out short vowel sounding words, eg. <u>c</u> <u>a</u> <u>t</u> , blending these phonemes to read the word, eg. cat.

Where is Sam's Ball?

Book 1

This is Sam. He is sad.

new words: Sam, **He, sad

He is sad and Mummy is sad.

new word: Mummy

Where is his ball.

new words: Where, his, ball

Here is his ball.

no new words

It is in the tree.

new words: **It, **in, **the, tree

Here is the tree and here is the ball.

no new words

It is in the tree.

no new words

Sam is sad his ball is in the tree.

no new words

Mummy is sad the ball is in the tree.

no new words

It is his ball. It is in the tree.

no new words

It is sad the ball is in the tree.

no new words

Sam wants the ball.

new word: wants

New words list

P.1   **He, sad

P.2   Mummy

P.3   Where, his, ball

P.4

P.5   **It, **in, **the, tree

P.6

P.7

P.8

P.9

P.10

P.11

P.12   wants

Sam's Cat

Book 2

Sam has a cat.

new words: has, **a, **cat

The cat has a ball.

new word: The

This is the ball. It is Sam's ball. The ball is here.

new word: Sam's

It is Sam's ball and it is Sam's cat.
Sam wants the ball.
This is my ball, says Sam.

new words: it, **my, says

Sam likes the ball. It is his ball.
Sam is happy his ball is not in the tree.

new words: likes, happy, not

It is not in the tree, says Sam. He is happy it is not in the tree.

The cat got the ball, says Sam.

Sam likes the cat. It is his cat.

new word: got

His cat is big and round.

new words: His, **big, round

Yes, it is big and round.

no new words

It looks like a big round orange.

new words: looks, orange

Yes, Sam's cat looks like a big round orange.

no new words

His name is Orange Pip.

new words: name, Orange Pip

New words list

P.1   has, **a, **cat

P.2   The

P.3   Sam's

P.4   it, **my, says

P.5   likes, happy, not

P.6   got

P.7   His, **big, round

P.8

P.9   looks, orange

P.10

P.11 name, Orange Pip

What Orange Pip Likes

Book 3

In the day, Orange Pip likes to sit.

new words: In, **day, **to, sit

In the day, Mummy likes to sit.

no new words

In the day, Daddy likes to sit.

new word: Daddy

In the day, Orange Pip likes to sit by Sam and Daddy.

new word: by

Mummy likes to sit by Sam.

no new words

Daddy likes to sit by Sam.

no new words

Sam likes to sit by the computer.

new word: computer

Daddy likes to sit by the computer. It is his computer.

no new words

Orange Pip likes to sit by Sam.

no new words

Sam likes to sit by Orange Pip.

no new words

Orange Pip likes to sit by Sam by the computer.

no new words

New words list

P.1　In, **day, **to, sit

P.2

P.3　Daddy

P.4　by

P.5

P.6

P.7　computer

P.8

P.9

P.10

P.11

Sam Goes on the Computer

Book 4

Sam likes to go on the computer.

new words; **go, **on

Orange Pip likes Sam to go on the computer.

no new words

In the day, Sam likes to read to Orange Pip.

new word: read

He likes to read to Mummy.

no new words

He likes to read to Daddy.

no new words

Sam loves to read to Orange Pip. He reads to Orange Pip like this.

    o x says ox

    o ff says off

    o n says on

    o dd says odd

Sound and say. This is an exercise encouraging short vowel sound phonic word recognition. Where double consonants occur explain that they make the same sound as a single consonant, but these words are greedy, they grab an extra letter for themselves, as in: e gg says egg but sounds the same as e g

new words: loves, reads

He reads to Mummy like this.

    a says a

    a t says at

    a m says am

    a n says an

Sound and say. This is an exercise encouraging short vowel sound phonic word recognition. Where double consonants occur explain that they make the same sound as a single consonant, but these words are greedy, they grab an extra letter for themselves, as in: e gg says egg but sounds the same as e g

no new words

He reads to Daddy like this.

    i n says in

    i t says it

    i s says is

    i ll says ill

Sound and say. This is an exercise encouraging short vowel sound phonic word recognition. Where double consonants occur explain that they make the same sound as a single consonant, but these words are greedy, they grab an extra letter for themselves, as in: e gg says egg but sounds the same as e g

no new words

Sam reads to Orange Pip for fun.

new words: **for, fun

Sam likes to read to Orange Pip for fun.

no new words

You read this with me, Orange Pip.

p i p says pip

p u p says pup

p o p says pop

p e t says pet

p a t says pat

Sound and say. This is an exercise encouraging short vowel sound phonic word recognition.

new words: **You, with, **me

You like to read with me.

no new words

Mummy likes to read with me, says Sam. It is good, says Mum.

new word: **Mum

Daddy likes to read with me, says Sam. It is good, says Dad.

new word: **Dad

New words list

P.1   **go, **on

P.2

P.3   read

P.4   by

P.5

P.6   loves, reads

P.7

P.8

P.9   **for, fun

P.10

P.11   **You, with, **me

P.12

P.13   **Mum

P.14   **Dad

Sam Teaches Orange Pip to Read

Book 5

You like to read with me, says Sam to Orange Pip. It is good.

no new words

You read this with me, Sam says. I will read this for you.

new word: will

You will sit by me and I will read for you.

no new words

You read this with me, he says.

    <u>d</u> <u>o</u> <u>g</u> says dog
    <u>c</u> <u>o</u> <u>t</u> says cot
    <u>m</u> <u>o</u> <u>p</u> says mop
    <u>t</u> <u>o</u> <u>p</u> says top
    <u>l</u> <u>o</u> <u>g</u> says log

Encouraging short vowel sound phonic recognition.

new word: *he

Good, says Sam. You read this with me.

<u>c</u> <u>u</u> <u>p</u> says cup
<u>h</u> <u>u</u> <u>t</u> says hut
<u>b</u> <u>u</u> <u>n</u> says bun
<u>t</u> <u>u</u> <u>b</u> says tub
<u>b</u> <u>u</u> <u>s</u> says bus

Encouraging short vowel sound phonic recognition.

new word: Good

Good, you read this with me, Sam says. That is good.

  <u>b</u> <u>i</u> <u>n</u> says bin
  <u>t</u> <u>i</u> <u>n</u> says tin
  <u>l</u> <u>i</u> <u>d</u> says lid
  <u>z</u> <u>i</u> <u>p</u> says zip
  <u>p</u> <u>i</u> <u>t</u> says pit

Encouraging short vowel sound phonic recognition.

new word: That

You are good, says Sam.
Read this with me.

p e t says pet

l e g says leg

h e n says hen

p a n says pan

p e n says pen

Encouraging short vowel sound phonic recognition.

new words: **are, Read

That is good, says Sam.
Read this with me.

<u>t a p</u> says tap

<u>b a g</u> says bag

<u>b a t</u> says bat

<u>f a t</u> says fat

<u>c a t</u> says cat

Encouraging short vowel sound phonic recognition.

no new words

<u>c</u> <u>a</u> <u>t</u> says cat. You are a cat, says Sam. You are not a dog.

new word: **dog

You are big and round. You are a big, round cat. You are not a dog.
Orange Pip says, meow.

new word: meow

New words list

P.1

P.2   will

P.3

P.4   **he

P.5   Good

P.6   That

P.7   are, Read

P.8

P.9   **dog

P.10 meow

Orange Pip is a Very Bad Cat

Book 6

You are big and round. You are a big, round cat. Sit here, says Sam. You sit here.

new word: Sit

You are a big orange cat, says Sam.

no new words

You are a very big orange cat, says Sam.

new word: very

Yes, you are a very big orange cat. You are very, very big.

no new words

Orange Pip says, meow.
Do this with me, says Sam.

no new words

Do this with me, says Sam.
Orange Pip says, meow, meow.

    <u>c</u> <u>a</u> <u>t</u> says cat

    <u>f</u> <u>a</u> <u>t</u> says fat

no new words

You are a very big fat cat, says Sam.

new word: fat

Orange Pip says, meow, meow, meow. He jumps up.

new words: jumps, **up

He jumps up and says, meow, meow, meow.

no new words

He jumps on the keyboard by the computer.

new word: keyboard

Orange Pip jumps up to the keyboard.

no new words

No, no, no, says Sam. Get down now. You get down now.

new words: no, **Get, **get, down, now

Get down now, says Sam.
No Orange Pip, get down, now.

no new words

You are a very bad cat, says Sam. Get down now and go away.

new words: bad, **away

Yes, go away, you are a very bad cat. The words went away.

new word: words, **went

You have made the words go away, says Sam. They went away. Get down now and go away.

new words: have, made, **They

New words list

P.1   Sit

P.2

P.3   very

P.4

P.5

P.6

P.7   fat

P.8   jumps, up

P.9

P.10 keyboard

P.11

P.12 no, **Get, **get, down, now

P.13

P.14 bad, **away

P.15 words, **went

P.16 have, made, **They

Orange Pip Runs Away

Book 7

You have made the words go away. You are a very bad cat, says Sam. I said you are a very bad cat.

new word: said

I will go away and call Mummy, says Sam. I said I will call Mummy.

new word: call

I will go away and call Daddy, says Sam.

no new words

Mummy says, I am here, do not do that.

new words: do, **am, that

Daddy says, I am here, do not do that.

no new words

What is this all about, says Mummy.

new words: What, all, about

What is this all about, says Daddy.

no new words

This is a very bad cat, says Mummy and Daddy.

no new words

Orange Pip gets down and runs away.

new words: gets, runs

New words list

P.1   **said

P.2   Call

P.3

P.4   do, **am, that

P.5

P.6   What, all, about

P.7

P.8

P.9   gets, runs

Orange Pip Hides in the Tree

Book 8

Orange Pip gets down and runs away.

no new words

Sam runs after him.

new words: after, him

Mummy runs after him.

no new words

Daddy runs after him.

no new words

You are a very bad cat, says Sam. I said you are bad. He throws his ball at Orange Pip.

new words: throws, **at

He throws his ball at Orange Pip. It lands in the tree.

new word: lands

Sam is sad. He wants his ball.

Here is the tree and here is the ball.

no new words

Orange Pip jumps up into the tree.

new word: into

He jumps into the tree.

no new words

Look at him now, says Sam. He is in the tree.

new word: **Look

Look at him now Mummy, says Sam. He is in the tree.

no new words

Look at him now, Daddy, says Sam. He is in the tree.

no new words

Come down here, says Sam to Orange Pip. You come down here.

new words: **Come, **come

Come down here, says Mummy to Orange Pip.
You come down here.

no new words

Come down here, says Daddy to Orange Pip. You come down here.
Orange Pip will not come down.

no new words

New words list

P.1

P.2   after, him

P.3

P.4

P.5   throws, **at

P.6   lands

P.7

P.8

P.9   into

P.10

P.11   Look

P.12

P.13

P.14   **Come, **come

P.15

P.16

Orange Pip is a Good Cat Now

Book 9

Sam is sad. His ball is in the tree. His cat is in the tree.

no new words

Orange Pip jumps on the ball in the tree to make it go down.

new word: make

You make it go down, says Sam.

no new words

You make it go down, says Daddy.

no new words

You make it go down, says Mummy.

Sam has the ball. You are a good cat, he says. You are not a bad cat now.

no new words

You are a very good cat now, says Sam.

no new words

You are a very good cat now, says Mummy.

no new words

You are a very good cat, now, says Daddy.

no new words

Look Mummy, says Sam.
This is my ball.

no new words

Look Daddy, says Sam.
This is my ball.

no new words

Sam is very happy now he has his ball.

no new words

Mummy is very happy that Sam has his ball.

no new words

Daddy is very happy that Sam has his ball.

no new words

New words list

P.1

P.2   make

P.3

P.4

P.5

P.6

P.7

P.8

P.9

P.10

P.11

P.12

P.13

P.14

Sam is Very Happy

Book 10

I love you Mummy. I love you Daddy. I love you Orange Pip, says Sam. Sam is happy. He has his ball.

no new words

Orange Pip says, meow. He jumps down and runs away. Sam is very happy. He runs after him.

no new words

Come back here Orange Pip, says Sam.

new word: back

Come back to the computer with me, says Sam. Come back and read with me.

no new words

Orange Pip runs away and Sam is very sad.

no new words

I will go back to the computer, says Sam. I will go on it.

no new words

I will read the words on it, says Sam.

no new words

Sam likes to go on the computer but he is sad.

new word: but

I love to read but I am sad, says Sam.

no new words

Sam is sad. He looks at the door. It is Orange Pip. Orange Pip says, meow. Orange Pip jumps up to the computer.

Orange Pip is here, Sam says to Mummy.

He has his ball and he has his cat.
Sam is happy now.

new word: door

Do this with me says Sam to Orange Pip. Do this with me and Mummy.

    <u>s</u> <u>h</u> says sh for ship
    Here is the ship.

    <u>s</u> <u>h</u> says sh for shop
    Here is the shop.

    <u>s</u> <u>h</u> says sh for shell
    Here is the shell.

s h says sh for shadow

Here is the shadow.

s h says sh for shunter

Here is the shunter.

Sound and say. This is an exercise encouraging recognition of consonant digraph sounds where two letters join to make a new sound. Encourage your child to sound each letter then explain when they join together they make a new sound. Discuss the meaning of the words then help your child to identify these digraph sounds as they occur anywhere in the text during the course of working through the next sections of the book.

no new words introduced for learning at this stage

Do this with me Orange Pip, says Sam. Do this with me.

<u>c</u> <u>h</u> says ch for chap
Here is the chap.

<u>c</u> <u>h</u> says ch for chestnut
Here is the chestnut.

<u>c</u> <u>h</u> says ch for chopstick
Here is the chopstick.

c̲ h̲ says ch for chicken

Here is the chicken

c̲ h̲ says ch for chum

He is my chum.

Sound and say. This is an exercise encouraging recognition of consonant digraph sounds where two letters join to make a new sound. Encourage your child to sound each letter then explain when they join together they make a new sound. Discuss the meaning of the words then help your child to identify these digraph sounds as they occur anywhere in the text during the course of working through the next sections of the book.

no new words introduced for learning at this stage

Do this with me, says Sam to Orange Pip. Do this with me and Mummy.

    t h says th for that
    Do we like that.

    t h says th for the
    Do we like the tree.

    t h says th for then
    This is for me then.

t h says th for there
Yes, there is the tree.

t h says th for this
Is this for you.

Sound and say. This is an exercise encouraging recognition of consonant digraph sounds where two letters join to make a new sound. Encourage your child to sound each letter then explain when they join together they make a new sound. Discuss the meaning of the words then help your child to identify these digraph sounds as they occur anywhere in the text during the course of working through the next sections of the book.

no new words introduced for learning at this stage

Do this with me Orange Pip, says Sam. Do this with me and Mummy.

q u says qu for queen
Here is the queen.

q u says qu for quiet
The queen is quiet.

q u says qu for quick
The queen is quick.

<u>q</u> <u>u</u> says qu for queue

The queen is in the queue.

<u>q</u> <u>u</u> says qu for quack

The duck says quack.

Sound and say. This is an exercise encouraging recognition of consonant digraph sounds where two letters join to make a new sound. Encourage your child to sound each letter then explain when they join together they make a new sound. Discuss the meaning of the words then help your child to identify these digraph sounds as they occur anywhere in the text during the course of working through the next sections of the book.

no new words introduced for learning at this stage

Do this with me Orange Pip, says Sam. Do this with me and Mummy.

    o o says oo as in moo
    The cow says moo.

    o w says ow as in cow
    Moo says the cow.

    o i says oi as in soil
    This is the soil.

o u says ou as in shout

I can shout.

e e says ee as in queen

The queen is here.

Sound and say. This is an exercise encouraging recognition of double vowel digraph sounds where two letters join to make a new sound. Encourage your child to sound each letter then explain how the sound changes when they are joined together to make a new sound. Discuss the meaning of the words then help your child to identify these vowel digraph sounds as they occur in the text, during the course of working through the next sections of the book. N.B. ow is included in this set.

no new words introduced for learning at this stage

Do this with me Orange Pip, says Sam. Do this with me and Mummy.

a i says ai as in paid
Mummy paid for this.

o a says oa as in boat
Here is the boat.

e a says ea as in beach

I love the beach.

Sound and say. This is an exercise encouraging recognition of consonant digraph sounds where two letters join to make a new sound. Encourage your child to sound each letter then explain when they join together they make a new sound. Discuss the meaning of the words then help your child to identify these digraph sounds as they occur anywhere in the text during the course of working through the next sections of the book.

no new words introduced for learning at this stage

Orange Pip jumps down. You are a very good cat, says Sam. You are a very good cat. I love you Orange Pip. I love you.

No new words

New words list

P.1

P.2

P.3   back

P.4

P.5

P.6

P.7

P.8   but

P.9

P.10   door

P.12   consonant digraph sound   sh

P.14   consonant digraph sound   sh

P.16   consonant digraph sound   ch

P.18   consonant digraph sound   ch

P.20   consonant digraph sound   th

P.22   consonant digraph sound   th

P.24   consonant digraph sound   qu

P.26   consonant digraph sound   qu

P.28   double vowel digraph sounds   oo, ow, oi

P.30   double vowel digraph sounds   ou, ee

P.32   double vowel digraph sounds   ai, oa

P.34   double vowel digraph sound   ea

P.36

Second series work guide:

In order to reinforce your child's understanding of the phonetic structure of words, before proceeding, please return to the Book 5 reader and the phonic word lists Sam introduces to the cat. Using the method described below work through each of the lists. You can turn it into a game by guessing which will be the longest list today as you both add new words to them at each session. Whilst the digraph sounds introduced in Book 15 are simply intended to extend phonic awareness, the example below shows how to deal with the teaching of this phonetic structure should you both, at a later stage wish to work through these lists in a similar way.

Single sound consonant/ short vowel sound three letter words should be introduced in the following way. Make two flashcards for each new word. Leave one whole and split the other word by cutting out each phoneme, eg. One of the cards that says the word

cat

should be cut into each phoneme (the smallest structure of sound) to make three cards, each with one component letter of the word, thus:

[c] [a] [t]

*Encourage your child to restructure the word against the other flashcard saying, 'Let's put the **c** back, now the **a**, **c**-**a**- , now the **t**, **c**-**a**-**t** says **cat**.' This will reinforce the understanding of the phonetic structure, (or element of the phonetic structure depending upon what's been identified in the word), whilst retaining the whole word recognition element. A further example being taken from the word:*

shout

Should be cut into each phoneme to make five cards, each with one component letter of the word, thus:

[s] [h] [o] [u] [t]

Return to the other flashcard pointing to the first two letters saying,'

'**s** *and* **h** *go together to make the sound* **sh**, *so let's put these two letters we've just cut out back in place on the whole word. Now point out that* **o** *and* **u** *go together to make the sound* **ou**, *saying,* '*So let's put these two letters we've just cut out back in place on the whole word, as well.*' *Then say,* '*Let's go back to the start of the word,* **s** *and* **h** *together says* **sh**, **o** *and* **u** *together says* **ou** *and (as you put it back, say) this last letter says* **t**. **sh**-**ou**-**t** *says* **shout**.' *Now make new cards for digraph sounds explaining that as* **s** *and* **h** *go together to make a new sound we can give them a card of their own, as with* **o** *and* **u** , *then replace these on the word.*

Work the next series of stories in exactly the same way as before. Read the page together using phonics where appropriate as a means of decoding new words.

Now help your child to draw a picture about the story after reading the words at the top of the page.

Repeat or write a short line on the bottom of the page taken from the words at the top then help your child to read this.

Continue to use the flashcards to sentence build, reinforcing any new words by working them with those your child already knows.

At the start check the words in the story for phonics listed by sounding out the phonic list at the bottom of each page, pointing out digraphs as they appear in the words. Where there are no matching sounds, move through the phonic line as appropriate for each page and work out a short sentence with your child to include one, eg. '*All about Sam*', *Page 2: You write:*

Sam is four.

I will be four shortly.

Work through this exercise in the manner described on the previous page to reinforce his/her appreciation of digraph sounds and give value to his/her own expression. Give liberal praise, date page and record progress in the 'Notes' section at the end of the book.

All About Sam

Book 11

This is Sam.

sh, ch, th, qu, oo, ow, oi, ou, ee, ai, oa, ea
no new words

Sam is four.

sh, ch, th, qu, oo, ow, oi, ou, ee, ai, oa, ea
new word: four

This is his Mummy.
I am four, he says to his Mummy. When will I be five.

sh, ch, th, qu, oo, ow, oi, ou, ee, ai, oa, ea
new words: am, When, be, five

When it is your birthday, says Mummy, you will be five.

sh, ch, th, qu, oo, ow, oi, ou, ee, ai, oa, ea
new words: your, birthday

This is his Daddy.

sh, ch, th, qu, oo, ow, oi, ou, ee, ai, oa, ea
no new words

This is his Aunty Sally.

sh, ch, th, qu, oo, ow, oi, ou, ee, ai, oa, ea
new words: Aunty, Sally

Aunty Sally shouts.

sh, ch, th, qu, oo, ow, oi, ou, ee, ai, oa, ea
new word: shouts

Sam does not like her.

sh, ch, th, qu, oo, ow, oi, ou, ee, ai, oa, ea
new words: does, her

This is his house. His house is big.

sh, ch, th, qu, oo, ow, oi, ou, ee, ai, oa, ea
new word: house

Sam likes his big house.

sh, ch, th, qu, oo, ow, oi, ou, ee, ai, oa, ea
no new words

It has a little garden at the front.

sh, ch, th, qu, oo, ow, oi, ou, ee, ai, oa, ea
new words: little, garden, front

It has a big garden at the back.

sh, ch, th, qu, oo, ow, oi, ou, ee, ai, oa, ea
no new words

New words list

P.1

P.2   four

P.3   am, When, be, five

P.4   your, birthday

P.5

P.6   Aunty, Sally

P.7   shouts

P.8   does, her

P.9   house

P.10

P.11   little, garden, front

P.12

Where Sam Lives

Book 12

Sam lives by the park.

sh, ch, th, qu, oo, ow, oi, ou, ee, ai, oa, ea
new words: lives, park

The park is at the back of his house.

sh, ch, th, qu, oo, ow, oi, ou, ee, ai, oa, ea
new word: **of

Sam can see the park at the back of his house. Sam likes it.

sh, ch, th, qu, oo, ow, oi, ou, ee, ai, oa, ea
new words: **can, see

When it is your birthday, says Mummy, you will be five.

sh, ch, th, qu, oo, ow, oi, ou, ee, ai, oa, ea
no new words

Sam likes living here.

sh, ch, th, qu, oo, ow, oi, ou, ee, ai, oa, ea
new word: living

He climbs the fence. He can see the children.

sh, ch, th, qu, oo, ow, oi, ou, ee, ai, oa, ea
new words: climbs, fence, children

He climbs the apple tree.
He can see the children.

sh, ch, th, qu, oo, ow, oi, ou, ee, ai, oa, ea
new word: apple

The children play ball.

sh, ch, th, qu, oo, ow, oi, ou, ee, ai, oa, ea
new word: **play

Sometimes the balls come into the garden. Sam throws them back.

sh, ch, th, qu, oo, ow, oi, ou, ee, ai, oa, ea
new words: Sometimes, balls, them

Mummy says, get down Sam.

sh, ch, th, qu, oo, ow, oi, ou, ee, ai, oa, ea
no new words

Daddy says, get down Sam.

Sam does not get down.

Aunty Sally shouts, get down Sam. Sam does not get down.

Sam does not like her.

sh, ch, th, qu, oo, ow, oi, ou, ee, ai, oa, ea
no new words

New words list

P.1   lives, park

P.2   **of

P.3   **can, see

P.4

P.5   living

P.6   climbs, fence, children

P.7   apple

P.8   **play

P.9   Sometimes, balls, throws

P.10

P.11

P.12

About the Park

Book 13

The park has swings.

sh, ch, th, qu, oo, ow, oi, ou, ee, ai, oa, ea
new word: swings

Sam likes the swings. I like the swings.

sh, ch, th, qu, oo, ow, oi, ou, ee, ai, oa, ea
no new words

The park has a slide.

sh, ch, th, qu, oo, ow, oi, ou, ee, ai, oa, ea
new word: slide

Sam likes the slide. I like the slide.

sh, ch, th, qu, oo, ow, oi, ou, ee, ai, oa, ea
no new words

The park has a big roundabout.

sh, ch, th, qu, oo, ow, oi, ou, ee, ai, oa, ea
new word: roundabout

Sam likes the big roundabout. I like the big roundabout.

sh, ch, th, qu, oo, ow, oi, ou, ee, ai, oa, ea
no new words

It goes round and round. It goes slow. It goes fast.

sh, ch, th, qu, oo, ow, oi, ou, ee, ai, oa, ea
new words: goes, slow, fast

Sam likes to go fast. I like to go fast. The roundabout likes to go fast.

sh, ch, th, qu, oo, ow, oi, ou, ee, ai, oa, ea
no new words

New words list

P.1　swings

P.2

P.3　slide

P.4

P.5　roundabout

P.6

P.7　goes, slow, fast

P.8

Sam Goes to the Park

Book 14

I want to go to the park, says Sam. Please can we go to the park Daddy, he says.

sh, ch, th, qu, oo, ow, oi, ou, ee, ai, oa, ea
new words: want, Please, **we

Daddy says, yes we will go to the park. We will go with Mummy.

sh, ch, th, qu, oo, ow, oi, ou, ee, ai, oa, ea
new words: **yes, We

Mummy says, yes we will go to the park. We will go with Daddy and Aunty Sally.

sh, ch, th, qu, oo, ow, oi, ou, ee, ai, oa, ea
no new words

Sam does not like Aunty Sally. He will throw his little black ball at her.

sh, ch, th, qu, oo, ow, oi, ou, ee, ai, oa, ea
new words: throw, black

Aunty Sally loves going to the park. She likes to shout at the children.

sh, ch, th, qu, oo, ow, oi, ou, ee, ai, oa, ea
new words: **going, **She, shout

Stop shouting, she says.
Stop fighting, she says.
The children do not like her.

sh, ch, th, qu, oo, ow, oi, ou, ee, ai, oa, ea
new words: Stop, shouting, **she, fighting

Aunty Sally meets them at the park. She is feeding the ducks.

sh, ch, th, qu, oo, ow, oi, ou, ee, ai, oa, ea
new words: meets, feeding, ducks

She goes on the slide but she is too big. She gets stuck.

sh, ch, th, qu, oo, ow, oi, ou, ee, ai, oa, ea
new words: too, stuck

She goes on the swing but she is too big. She gets stuck.

sh, ch, th, qu, oo, ow, oi, ou, ee, ai, oa, ea
new word: swing

She goes on the roundabout but she is too big. It will not go round and round.

sh, ch, th, qu, oo, ow, oi, ou, ee, ai, oa, ea
no new words

All the children shout, get off, but she will not get off.

sh, ch, th, qu, oo, ow, oi, ou, ee, ai, oa, ea
new words: **All, off

New words list

P.1   want, Please, **we

P.2   **yes, We

P.3

P.4   throw, black

P.5   **going, **She, shout

P.6   Stop, shouting, she, fighting

P.7   meets, feeding, ducks

P.8   too, stuck

P.9   swing

P.10

P.11 **All, off

Sam Gets into Trouble

Book 15

Sam is bored. He throws his little black ball high into the sky. It bounces high. It bounces low.

sh, ch, th, qu, oo, ow, oi, ou, ee, ai, oa, ea
new words: bored, bounces, high, sky, low

It bounces high into the sky. It bounces high then goes plop into the water, splashing Aunty Sally all over.

sh, ch, th, qu, oo, ow, oi, ou, ee, ai, oa, ea
new words: then, water, plop, splashing, over

Aunty Sally shouts. She is very cross with Sam. All the children are laughing. They laugh at Aunty Sally.
That ball is splashing me all over, she shouts.

sh, ch, th, qu, oo, ow, oi, ou, ee, ai, oa, ea
new words: cross, laughing, laugh

She goes home. Mummy and Daddy are cross with Sam.

sh, ch, th, qu, oo, ow, oi, ou, ee, ai, oa, ea
new word: home

It was the little black ball, not me, Sam says. I have lost it now.

sh, ch, th, qu, oo, ow, oi, ou, ee, ai, oa, ea
new words: **was, lost

I have lost my little black ball, says Sam. Please can I have the big red ball now. It is in the shop, he says.

sh, ch, th, qu, oo, ow, oi, ou, ee, ai, oa, ea
new word: Please, red, shop

No, you must wait for your birthday but you must be a very good boy, says Mummy.

sh, ch, th, qu, oo, ow, oi, ou, ee, ai, oa, ea
new words: must, wait, boy

Yes, you will get it for your birthday but only if you are a very good boy, says Daddy.

sh, ch, th, qu, oo, ow, oi, ou, ee, ai, oa, ea
new words: only, if

You must promise to be nice to Aunty Sally, says Mummy.

sh, ch, th, qu, oo, ow, oi, ou, ee, ai, oa, ea
new words: promise, nice

You must promise to be nice to Aunty Sally, says Daddy.

sh, ch, th, qu, oo, ow, oi, ou, ee, ai, oa, ea
no new words

I promise, says Sam.

I do not like Aunty Sally. I will not want to throw my big red ball at her.

He knows she will throw it in the water.

Sam knows he will not want to lose his big red ball like that.

sh, ch, th, qu, oo, ow, oi, ou, ee, ai, oa, ea
new words: knows, lose

New words list

P.1   bored, bounce, high, sky, low

P.2   then, water, plop, splashing, over

P.3   cross, laughing, laugh

P.4   home

P.5   **was, lost

P.6   Please, red, shop

P.7   must, wait, boy

P.8   only, if

P.9   promise, nice

P.10

P.11 knows, lose

Guide page

The 45 NLS key words have now been introduced and identified thus ** in the previous 15 readers. Just to remind you, in helping your child with the reading of each of these stories, it is recommended giving additional reinforcement to these words for although children will not be required to know them all until the end of Key Stage One, focussing on them during the course of working through this book, at their, own pace, will certainly help in the achievement of this. As previously mentioned, they will also be expected to bring to school a knowledge of short vowel sounds and initial and final sounds in words, so it is worth spending some time on this, working within the phonic framework introduced here.

Although the concluding story may simply be read to your child in order to find out what happens to Sam, you may like to work through it with him/her, encouraging the deployment of phonic skills where appropriate in the learning of new words. Help your child by writing the letters down as you hear him/her making the sounds, then blend the sounds to make the word. Using your pen allow him/her to trace over your letters, ensuring the correct pen hold and the correct letter formation.

Please remember, however, this book goes well beyond foundation level and should always be worked at your child's own pace. Use it to suit the needs of your child and consider enjoyment the priority as she reads, writes, draws and colours, to make this book his/her own. This is the most valuable achievement of all, for in doing so your child will be intrinsically motivated to learn and you can be justly proud of having provided the best possible foundation for developing the basic skills needed in learning to read.

Sam and Billy Ball

Sam lives by the park. Sometimes Mummy takes him to the park. Sam likes to play ball with his friends.

Sam's house

This is his house. It is big. It has a long garden at the back. At the bottom of the garden is a big apple tree.

Sam can see the fence. Sometimes Sam climbs the fence. He can see the children playing in the park.

The slide

They play on the slide.

The swings

They play on the swings.

The roundabout

They play on the roundabout.

The climbing frame

They play on the climbing frame.

Sam always goes there first. The climbing frame is his favourite place to play.

Sam loves climbing. He climbs up the stairs. He climbs on the bed. He jumps on the bed. Mummy shouts. She tells him not to do it but Sam always forgets.

Sam is five today. It is his birthday. Mummy and Daddy give him the big red ball. Sam loves the ball. He calls it Billy.

Billy Ball has a happy face. Billy Ball has two eyes that can see. Billy Ball has one nose that can breathe. Billy Ball has one mouth that can speak. Billy Ball has two ears that can hear. Billy Ball is magic but Sam does not know this.

Today Sam is having a birthday party. It is bad for Sam. He knows Aunty Sally will kiss him.

The birthday cake

Mummy and Aunty Sally bring in the cake. It has five candles on it. Sam and his friends watch them being lit. Billy Ball bounces up and down so he can see. Orange Pip runs away. He does not like Billy Ball.

Mummy tells Sam to stop playing with the ball. Sam tries to catch it but it bounces high and low and high again. It lands on the birthday cake and blows the candles out.

Sam and the children laugh. Sam grabs the ball. It is covered in icing. Mummy wants to wash it but Sam says, no. Aunty Sally wants to wash it but Sam says, no. Daddy wants to wash it but Sam says, no. He runs into the garden and throws it into the apple tree. All the children watch.

Sam is laughing. He looks at the fence. At the bottom he sees some balls sitting in the grass. They have come from the park. He counts them, one, two, three. They are smaller than his big red ball.

He picks up the yellow ball. He throws it at the tree but it will not make his big red ball come down. It gets stuck.

He picks up the blue ball. He throws it at the tree but it will not make his big red ball come down. It gets stuck.

He picks up the green ball. He throws it at the tree but it will not make his big red ball come down. It gets stuck.

Sam can see the balls. He counts them, one, two, three, four. Sam wants the balls. He climbs the tree all the way to the top. He can see Mummy and Aunty Sally. He can see Daddy as well but he can not see Orange Pip.

Mummy is holding a wet cloth. She wants to wipe the big red ball clean.

Aunty Sally is holding a wet cloth. She wants to wipe the big red ball clean. They tell Sam to come down. Aunty Sally is shouting in a very loud voice.

Aunty Sally is shouting

Sam does not like Aunty Sally. He grabs the big red ball. Sam is surprised. The big red ball is smiling at him. It is sticking its tongue out.

Sam sees it has one big long red tongue to lick with. The big long red tongue has licked the icing from its face. Now Sam is happy. He knows Billy Ball is magic.

Aunty Sally is still shouting at Sam. She is telling him to come down.

Sam throws the sticky red ball down.

It lands in the grass

It bounces on her head then off again to land in the grass. She waves her finger at Sam. She is very cross.

Sam throws the little yellow ball down. It hits her on the nose and bounces into her mouth. It gets stuck. She can not speak. She waves her finger at Sam. She is very cross.

Sam throws the little blue ball down but it hits Mummy instead.

Sam throws the little green ball down but it hits Daddy instead.

Mummy and Daddy and Aunty Sally are very cross. All the children are laughing.

Aunty Sally can not speak

Mummy wipes the sticky red ball with the wet cloth but she sees the icing has disappeared.

Mummy is cross

Daddy wipes the sticky red ball with the wet cloth but he sees the icing has disappeared. They want to know where the icing has gone.

Daddy wipes the ball

Mummy looks at Sam. It is not on his top. Daddy looks at Sam. It is not on his top. Aunty Sally looks at Sam. It is not on his top.

The big red ball jumps at Aunty Sally and lands on her chin. The little yellow ball shoots from her mouth and lands on the grass.

This naughty boy has sat in the tree and licked it all off, she says.

Sam says, It was not me, it was the big red ball. It is a magic ball.

Sam looks at Aunty Sally. Her big round face is red. She looks like Billy Ball.

Now he is telling fibs. Send him to bed she says. He is a naughty boy. Give that ball to me now.

Aunty Sally grabs the big red ball but it jumps up and down in her hands. She tries to drop it but it will not let go. I am going home she says. Get away from me you horrible thing.

She runs down the garden. She runs down the path. She runs to the front gate.

Mummy runs after her. Daddy runs after her. Sam runs after her. All the children run after her. She gets in her car. She drives away with the big red ball sitting on the top.

The ball is on the car roof

Mummy is puzzled because the big red ball does not fall off the roof of the car.

It was very sticky but I wiped it clean, she says.

There must have been some sticky icing left on it, says Daddy. It is not a magic ball.

It is, it is, says Sam. I want it back.

If it is magic, says Daddy it will come back all by itself.

Mummy and Daddy laugh.

When bed time comes all the children go home. Sam climbs the stairs. He is feeling very sad. He wants Billy Ball back. He gets into bed. He wants Orange Pip back, too.

Good night Sam says Mummy.

Good night Sam says Daddy. We will get your big red ball back tomorrow. Go to sleep now.

Sam closes his eyes. Then he turns over.

He feels something big and round by his side.

He feels something long and wet on his cheek.

Yuk what was that. He grabs the big red ball and throws it down to the floor.

Aunty Sally does that to Mummy.

Aunty Sally does that to Daddy.

Yuk. Aunty Sally does that to me, he says.

The big red ball starts to cry. I am going back to the tree, it says, bouncing out of the room.

Sam hides in the bed covers and closes his eyes to go to sleep. Then he remembers the big red ball teaching Aunty Sally a lesson. Sam feels bad. He wants the big red ball to come back. He wants to say sorry.

Sam closes his eyes. Then he turns over. He feels something big and round by his side. It is the big red ball back again.

Sam is so happy he gives the sticky red ball a kiss. You taste nice, he says. He kisses it again.

Yuk, I can feel something long and wet on my cheek, says the big red ball. Stop licking me. I am going back to the tree, he says, and this time I will not come back.

Orange Pip jumps up and licks his face. Yuk, says Sam but he is happy. He has Orange Pip back and he knows Billy Ball will still be in the tree in the morning. But best of all, he knows he has a new magic friend that does not like being kissed either.

Flashcard Word List

*Frequently used words
**NLS key words for learning

a
**------------------------

about
*------------------------

after
*------------------------

again

All
**------------------------

all
**------------------------

always
----

am
**------------------------

an
----

and
**------------------------

apple
----

are
**------------------------

as

At
**------------------------

at
**------------------------

Aunty
----

away
**------------------------

back
*------------------------

bad	blows
Ball	blue
ball	bored
balls	bottom
be	bounces
*because	bouncing
bed	boy
been	breathe
being	bring
best	but*
big	by*
**Billy Ball	cake
birthday	call*
black	calls

came	cloth
Can	Come
**can	**come
**candles	comes
car	computer
cat	could
**catch	counts
cheek	covered
children	covers
chin	cross
clean	cry
climbing	Dad
climbs	**Daddy
closes	*day
	**

did	either
disappeared	eyes
Do *	face
do *	fall
Does	fast
does	fat
dog **	favourite
door	feeding
down *	feeling
drives	feels
drop	fence
ducks	fibs
ears	fighting
eggs	finger

| first |
| five |
| floor |
| for **|
| forgets |
| four |
| frame |
| friend |
| friends |
| from |
| front |
| fun |
| garden |
| gate |

| Get ** |
| get ** |
| gets * |
| Give |
| give |
| gives |
| Go |
| go ** |
| goes * |
| going ** |
| gone |
| Good |
| good |
| got * |

grabs	her
------------------------	*------------------------
grass	Here
------------------------	*------------------------
green	here
------------------------	*------------------------
had	hides
------------------------	------------------------
hands	high
------------------------	------------------------
happy	him
------------------------	*------------------------
has	His
*------------------------	*------------------------
have	his
*------------------------	*------------------------
having	hit
------------------------	------------------------
He	hits
**------------------------	------------------------
he	holding
**------------------------	------------------------
head	home
------------------------	------------------------
hear	horrible
------------------------	------------------------
Her	house
------------------------	------------------------

How	keyboard
*_____	_____
I	kiss
**_____	_____
icing	kissed
_____	_____
If	kisses
_____	_____
In	know
_____	_____
in	knows
**_____	_____
instead	land
_____	_____
into	lands
*_____	_____
is	last
**_____	_____
It	laugh
**_____	_____
it	laughing
**_____	_____
its	left
_____	_____
itself	lesson
_____	_____
jumps	let
_____	_____

lick	looks
licking	* lose
licked	lost
licks	loud
like	love
** likes	loves
* lit	low
little	made
* live	* magic
lives	make
living	* me
long	** meets
Look	meow
** look	morning
**	

mouth	not
----------------	*----------------
Mum	Now
**----------------	----------------
Mummy	now
*----------------	*----------------
must	of
----------------	**----------------
my	off
**----------------	*----------------
name	old
----------------	----------------
naughty	on
----------------	**----------------
new	once
----------------	----------------
next	one
----------------	*----------------
nice	only
----------------	----------------
night	orange
----------------	----------------
No	Orange Pip
**----------------	----------------
no	oranges
**----------------	----------------
nose	other
----------------	----------------

our	put
out	puzzled
over	Read
*	
park	read
party	reads
path	red
picks	remember
place	roof
play	room
**	
playing	round
*	
Please	roundabout
please	run
plop	runs
	*
promise	sad

said **	shout
Sally	shouting
Sam	shouts
Sam's	side
sat	Sit
saw	sit
say	sitting
says *	sky
see **	sleep
sees *	slide
Send	slow
She **	smaller
she **	smiling
shop	so

some	stuck
something	surprised
Sometimes	swing
sorry	swings
speak	take
splashing	takes
stairs	taste
starts	teaching
stay	tell
sticking	telling
sticky	tells
still	than
Stop	That *
stop	that *

The	throw
**_____	_____
the	throws
**_____	_____
their	time
_____	_____
them	to
*_____	**_____
Then	today
*_____	_____
then	tomorrow
_____	_____
There	tongue
*_____	_____
there	too
*_____	_____
They	top
**_____	_____
they	tree
**_____	_____
thing	tries
_____	_____
This	turns
**_____	_____
this	two
**_____	_____
three	under
_____	_____

up **	we **
us	well
very *	went **
voice	were
wait	wet
want *	What *
wants *	what
was **	When *
wash	when
watch	Where *
water	where
waves	will *
way	wipe
We **	wiped

wipes
---
with
*---
words

Yellow

Yes
**---
yes
**---

You
**---
you
**---
Your
---
your
*---
yours

Yuk

Flashcards for cutting

a

about

after

again

All

all

always

am

an

and

apple

are

as

At

at

Aunty

away

back

bad

Ball

ball

balls

be

because

bed

been

being

best

big

Billy Ball

birthday

black

blows

blue

bored

bottom

bounces

bouncing

boy

breathe

bring

but

by

cake

call

calls

came

Can

can

---

candles

---

car

---

cat

---

catch

---

cheek

---

children

---

chin

---

clean

climbing

climbs

closes

cloth

Come

come

comes

computer

could

counts

covered

covers

cross

cry

Dad

Daddy

day

did

disappeared

Do

do

Does

does

dog

door

down

drives

drop

ducks

ears

eggs

either

eyes

face

fall

fast

fat

favourite

feeding

feeling

---

feels

---

fence

---

fibs

---

fighting

---

finger

---

first

---

five

---

floor

for

forgets

four

frame

friend

friends

from

front

fun

garden

gate

Get

get

gets

Give

give

gives

Go

go

goes

going

gone

Good

good

got

grabs

grass

green

had

hands

happy

has

have

having

He

he

head

hear

Her

her

Here

here

hides

high

him

His

his

hit

hits

holding

home

horrible

house

How

I

icing

If

In

in

instead

into

is

It

it

its

itself

jumps

keyboard

kiss

kissed

kisses

know

knows

land

lands

last

laugh

laughing

left

lesson

let

lick

licking

licked

licks

like

likes

lit

little

live

lives

living

long

Look

look

looks

lose

lost

loud

love

loves

low

made

magic

make

me

meets

meow

morning

mouth

Mum

Mummy

must

my

name

naughty

new

next

nice

night

No

no

nose

not

Now

now

of

off

---

old

---

on

---

once

---

one

---

only

---

orange

Orange Pip

---

oranges

other

our

out

over

park

party

path

picks

place

play

playing

Please

please

plop

promise

put

puzzled

Read

read

reads

red

remember

roof

room

round

roundabout

run

runs

sad

said

Sally

Sam

Sam's

sat

saw

say

says

see

sees

Send

She

she

shop

shout

shouting

shouts

side

Sit

sit

sitting

sky

sleep

slide

slow

smaller

smiling

so

some

something

Sometimes

sorry

speak

splashing

stairs

starts

stay

sticking

sticky

still

Stop

stop

stuck

surprised

swing

swings

take

takes

taste

teaching

tell

telling

tells

than

That

that

The

the

their

them

Then

then

There

there

They

they

thing

This

this

three

throw

throws

time

to

today

tomorrow

tongue

too

top

tree

tries

turns

two

under

up

us

very

voice

wait

want

wants

was

wash

watch

water

waves

way

We

we

---

well

---

went

---

were

---

wet

What

---

what

When

---

when

Where

---

where

---

will

---

wipe

---

wiped

---

wipes

---

with

---

words

Yellow

Yes

---

yes

You

---

you

Your

---

yours

Yuk

Flashcard blanks

References

House of Commons: Education and Skills Committee: Teaching Children to Read: Eighth Report of Session 2004-05. HC 121 Incorporating HC 1269-I from Session 2003-04. Published 7 April 2005 by authority of the House of Commons, London: the Stationery Office Limited
Attribution statements cited from the above Report in the Foreward to this work are done so under the Open Government Licence for public sector information.

Ofsted: 'Getting them reading early': Distance learning materials for inspecting reading within the new framework: Ref. No. 110122 Published by Ofsted October 2011.
In respect of the above Guidance, the Introduction to this book contains public sector information licensed under the Open Government Licence V1.0.

Department for Education: Statutory Framework for the Early Years Foundation Stage: setting the standards for learning, development and care for children from birth to five. Published by the Department for Education 27 March 2012
In respect of the above Statutory Framework the Introduction to this work contains public sector information under the Open Government Licence V1.0.
Whilst the Author considers some of the work to be compatible with the Department for Education: Early Years Foundation Stage content, it has not been endorsed by them or anyone to whom in respect of the above, an attribution statement has been made.

http://www.education.gov.uk/schools/teachingandlearning/curriculum Corporate Author: Department for Education: Schools Teaching and Learning: The School Curriculum: Primary Curriculum Subjects English: En2 Reading
In respect of the above Primary Curriculum, the Crown body, The Department for Education permits reproduction under the terms of the Open Government Licence. The introduction to this book and the second part of this book contains public sector information licensed under the Open Government Licence.

www.early-education.org.uk: Early Education: The British Association for Early Childhood Education: Development Matters in the Early Years Foundation Stage (EYFS): This non-statutory guidance material supports practitioners in implementing the statutory requirements of the EYFS. Published, n.d.

National Foundation for Educational Research: Brooks, Greg. Trends in standards of literacy in the United Kingdom, 1948-1996
 http://www.leeds.ac.uk/educol/documents/000000650.htm

Much of the information included in this work is believed to be 'common knowledge' and its source is many and varied. Whilst there has been no verbatim use of copy, it is possible that some has been gleaned from publications such as:

The British Psychological Society: ongoing monthly publications: The Psychologist, recipient member over a number of years, including:
Solity, Jonathan and Shapiro, Laura R. Developing the Practice of Educational Psychologists through Theory and Research. Educational & Child Psychology: Vol 25 No 3 The British Psychological Society (2008)
Seth, G. Personality Growth and Learning. British Journal of Educational Psychology, 43192-197 (1973)
Faulkner, D, et al. Working With Under Fives: An in-Service Training Pack (Professional Development in Education) The Open University (1991) 1997
Open University (Faculty of Educational Studies): Course E281 (1979)
Bynner, John, et al. (The Personality Growth and Learning Course Team)
Personality Growth and Learning: a source book: Longman for the Open university Press 1971
Bowlby, John. Childcare and the Growth of Love: Penguin 1965
Holt, J. How Children fail: Penguin Books, new rev.ed 1990
Vernon, M. D. Human Motivation: Cambridge University Press 1969
Vernon, P. E. Personality Assessment: Methuen & Co 1966

The Author wishes to thank Guardian News & Media Ltd for their kind permission to refer to Author, Katherine Demopoulos' article " 'Children 'need 1000 key words' to read" published online 09/12/05

My grateful thanks and appreciation to Richard Franklin, Director of arima publishing for his unfailing help and patience in getting this work to print.

Also I wish to express my gratitude to designer Pete Franklin for the cover work and formatting the contents to perfection.

Notes

www.ingramcontent.com/pod-product-compliance
Lightning Source LLC
Chambersburg PA
CBHW081341230426
43667CB00017B/2696